BIBLE STUDY COMMENTARY

1 Peter–Revelation

Bible Study Commentary

1 Peter — Revelation

PAUL GARDNER

Scripture Union
130, City Road, London EC1V 2NJ

CHRISTIAN LITERATURE CRUSADE
Fort Washington, Pennsylvania 19034

© 1988 Paul Gardner
130 City Road, London EC1V 2NJ

First published 1988

ISBN 0 86201 368 2 (UK)
ISBN 0 87508 175 4 (USA)

Maps: Jenny Grayston

Phototypeset in Great Britain by Wyvern Typesetting Limited,
Central Trading Estate, 277 Bath Road, Bristol BS4 3EH

Printed in Great Britain by Ebenezer Baylis & Son Limited,
The Trinity Press, Worcester, and London.

Contents

General Introduction

The world-wide church in the last quarter of the twentieth century faces a number of challenges. In some places the church is growing rapidly and the pressing need is for an adequately trained leadership. Some Christians face persecution and need support and encouragement while others struggle with the inroads of apathy and secularism. We must come to terms, too, with the challenges presented by Marxism, Humanism, a belief that 'science' can conquer all the ills of mankind, and a whole range of Eastern religions and modern sects. If we are to make anything of this confused and confusing world it demands a faith which is solidly biblical.

Individual Christians, too, in their personal lives face a whole range of different needs – emotional, physical, psychological, mental. As we think more and more about our relationships with one another in the body of Christ and as we explore our various ministries in that body, as we discover new dimensions in worship and as we work at what it means to embody Christ in a fallen world we need a solid base. And that base can only come through a relationship with Jesus Christ which is firmly founded on biblical truth.

The Bible, however, is not a magical book. It is not enough to say, 'I believe', and quote a few texts selected at random. We must be prepared to work with the text until our whole outlook is moulded by it. We must be ready to question our existing position and ask the true meaning of the word for us in our situation. All this demands careful study not only of the text but also of its background and of our culture. Above all it demands prayerful and expectant looking to the Spirit of God to bring the word home creatively to our own hearts and lives.

This new series of books has been commissioned in response to the repeated requests for something new to follow on from Bible Characters and Doctrines. It is now over ten years since the first series of Bible Study Books was produced and it is hoped they will reflect the changes of the last ten years and bring the Bible text to life for a new generation of readers.

The series has three aims:

1. To encourage regular, systematic, personal Bible reading. Each volume is divided into sections ideally suited to daily use, and will normally provide material for three months (the exceptions being Psalms, four months, and Mark and Ezra–Job, two months). Used in this way the books will cover the entire Bible in five years. The comments aim to give background information and enlarge on the meaning of the text, with special reference to the contemporary relevance. Detailed questions of application are, however, often left to the reader. The questions for further study are designed to aid in this respect.

2. To provide a resource manual for group study. These books do not provide a detailed plan for week by week study. Nor do they present a

group leader with a complete set of ready-made questions or activity ideas. They do, however, provide the basic biblical material and, in the questions for further discussion, they give starting points for group discussion.

3. To build into a complete Bible commentary. There is, of course, no shortage of commentaries. Here, however, we have a difference. Rather than look at the text verse by verse the writers examine larger blocks of text, preserving the natural flow of the original thought and observing natural breaks.

Writers have based their comments on the RSV and some have also used the New International Version in some detail. The books can, however, be used with any version.

1 Peter: Introduction

The letters of James, 1 and 2 Peter, 1, 2, and 3 John and Jude are usually known as the 'catholic epistles'. This simply means that (with the exception of 2 and 3 John) they were addressed to the church world-wide rather than to specific local situations.

1 Peter is more specific in giving its destination than the others. It was written 'to God's elect, strangers in the world, scattered throughout Pontus, Galatia, Cappadocia, Asia and Bithynia' (1:1 NIV). These places denote Roman provinces in Turkey (Pontus and Bithynia being administered as a single province; see map, p 13). It is impossible to know how widely the letter was distributed in these provinces but it is possible that the letter was a circular one carried from place to place.

Authorship
Although some scholars have suggested that the letter was not written by Peter it does claim to be written by the apostle (1:1), and there are substantial reasons why this may be accepted as correct.

1. There are several thoughts and even phrases which bring to mind the speeches of Peter given in Acts. See, for example, 1:10 (Acts 2:16–17,29–31); 1:20 (Acts 2:23); 2:7 (Acts 4:11–12); 2:24 (Acts 5:30; 10:39); 4:5 (Acts 10:42).

2. There are allusions to incidents described in the Gospels in which Peter himself played a prominent role. For examples, see the comments below on 2:13–17; 2:25; 5:2; 5:10.

3. The early church fathers raise no question concerning either its authorship or its value to the church. It is possible that the letter was even known to Clement of Rome when he wrote to the Corinthians at the end of the first century.

However, in spite of these points it has been suggested that, because the Greek in which the letter was written is fluent and polished, it could hardly have been written by an 'uneducated' and ignorant man like Peter (Acts 4:13). In response to this it should be noted that the context of Acts 4:13 is polemic. The 'rulers and elders and scribes' (v 5) were accusing Peter and John, and it is in contrast with these ruling officials that they are described as 'uneducated'. A M Stibbs has suggested that the word for 'uneducated' used in Acts implies not so much illiteracy as 'laymen' with regard to matters of Scripture and religion.

Closely related to this discussion is the suggestion that Silvanus may have written the letter. This Silvanus was probably the 'Silas' who travelled with Paul on the second missionary journey and is mentioned on a number of occasions in Acts 15–18. Paul mentions 'Silvanus' in 1 Thessalonians 1:1, 2 Thessalonians 1:1, and 2 Corinthians 1:19. This suggestion arises from 5:12 where we read (literally): 'By Silvanus, to you a faithful brother (as I regard him), I have written briefly to you...' It may mean simply that Silvanus carried the letter to the readers. On the other hand, it may well mean that Peter used Silvanus as his amanuensis. The fact that he has 'written briefly' by Silvanus rather than 'sent' the letter by him suggests that such was the case.

The use of a 'secretary' in this way was certainly not unknown in the first century (compare Rom 16:22). At times such writers were given considerable freedom in how they wrote provided they communicated the message required. If Peter used Silvanus in this way then it would be Silvanus who produced the polished Greek, but Peter who watched over the message and confirmed the contents to be his (Peter's) message.

Place

Peter almost certainly wrote this epistle from Rome. We may deduce this from the following:

1. 5:13 refers to 'Babylon', a metaphorical name for Rome. (See Rev 17:4–6,9,18, esp. verse 9 where the seven mountains must be the seven hills on which Rome is built. Babylon in Mesopotamia is on a plain.) Babylon in Mesopotamia had been regarded as the evil centre of idolatry by Jews. In Peter's day Rome had assumed that position, so the use of the name Babylon is a metaphorical description of the city that was the centre of evil.

2. Mark is also mentioned in 5:13. We know from other sources that he lived in Rome (see Col 4:10).

3. The order in which the provinces are listed in 1:1 suggests travel eastwards from Rome, on a circuit that eventually came back towards the west.

4. Finally, it is very widely and traditionally accepted that Peter did end his ministry in Rome.

The recipients

The opening verse of the epistle refers to 'exiles of the Dispersion'. 2:12 refers to the recipients maintaining 'good conduct among the Gentiles', and in 4:3 Peter contrasts the behaviour of the Gentiles with what is expected of those to whom he is writing. The Greek fathers, Calvin, and others have therefore assumed that the intended recipients of the letter were converts from Judaism. The strong appeals to the Old Testament might also support this view. However, the majority of modern commentators point to other references that indicate the opposite. It is hardly conceivable, they argue, that Jews would have practised idolatry in Peter's day, and yet 4:3 refers to such practice. Further it is said that Peter would hardly have described their fathers' life which they have inherited as 'futile' (1:18) had they been of Jewish origin. And could Jews be described as formerly 'no people' but now 'God's people' (2:10)? Thus it is said the recipients were predominantly Gentile.

The arguments, it seems, can go both ways and are referred to briefly in the later discussion of the texts. However, a good case can still be made for the idea that Peter was writing to a group that were predominantly converted Jews.

Persecutions

A theme which appears throughout the letter is that of persecution and suffering. Discussion of the importance of this theme and the type of persecution Peter has in mind has occupied pages upon pages in commentaries. There are two important reasons for trying to understand what sort of persecution is involved.

1. It will affect our dating of the epistle, especially if it seems that it refers to empire-wide persecutions of Christians.

2. It will influence the way we think about the theological emphases in the epistle and, therefore, how we may apply the text legitimately to our own experience in the late twentieth century.

Those who doubt that Peter wrote the letter usually date it either in the time of the persecution of Christians under the emperor Domitian (AD 81–96), or in the time of Trajan (AD 98–117). However, if we assume that Peter wrote the epistle and accept the traditional understanding that he died under the Neronian persecution in AD 63 or 64, then it is quite possible that Peter was foreseeing trouble for Christians in the provinces – trouble that had already begun in Rome. Even so, he may not have had official state persecution in mind.

The evidence is far from conclusive and is referred to later in comments on the text. General suffering is certainly envisaged (see 1:6; 2:12; 3:13–17; 4:12–19). However, 4:12 seems, at first glance, to indicate a greater sense of urgency with an impending 'fiery ordeal'. Does this therefore refer to some emperor's edict against Christians? Possibly so, but in fact it is easy to make too much of the apparent change in emphasis at 4:12; the images of 'testing', 'fire' and suffering as a criminal have already been used earlier in the letter (1:7; 2:19–25; 3:17).

E G Selwyn and C F D Moule have both argued that nothing more need be envisaged by Peter than the local ridicule, and occasional battles with the authorities, that Christians have known ever since the day of Pentecost. 'The persecution presupposed in 1 Peter seems not to have originated from an imperial ban on Christianity, for Peter still speaks of the governor as a protector (3:13; 2:13–17). The empire-wide ban came later. The persecution rather took the form of slanderous accusations, social ostracism, mob riots and local police action.' (Gundry.) It is assumed in the commentary below that Peter wrote the epistle, probably towards the end of his life, in the early sixties AD.

Purpose and teaching

Peter's purpose in writing this epistle may be defined quite straightforwardly. During a time of general suffering and persecution he writes to encourage Christians to keep the promise of salvation before them (1:3–5). He tells them how to behave as Christians and shows them the right perspective from which to view their suffering.

In doing all this Peter touches upon various deep and valuable theological ideas, some of which may have been known in the early churches in the form of a catechism. Parallels between this letter and 1 and 2 Thessalonians in particular support this view. In other words, Peter expands his thoughts by teaching more clearly the truths of the Christian faith so well-known in the churches where the apostles and their followers had preached.

Outline

Chapter 1 joyfully reminds the readers of the great doctrines of grace. By God's great mercy men and women are saved and kept for Christ at the last day. Christ is the means of redemption.

Chapters 2 and 3 pick up the theme already introduced in chapter 1: that such graciousness requires a response, for these people are a 'spiritual house' of which Christ is the cornerstone. The response is to be seen in the lives of believers.

Chapter 4 begins with the example of Christ's sufferings, then turns to his judgment over wickedness. But God has prepared his people for life in this world with gifts with which they should look after each other and honour him. Suffering and ordeals of various sorts must be seen in the light of his faithfulness.

Chapter 5 reminds elders of their particular responsibilities and again urges watchfulness and a complete reliance upon the Lord. Through suffering, the 'God of all grace' will be seen in his full saving and restoring glory.

The epistle therefore becomes a masterful combination of encouragement to right living in a time of suffering, and of teaching centred around the graciousness of God revealed in Christ as Saviour and as example.

Application

This commentary is written with a view to learning from the text and then applying it in our lives. Sometimes questions are raised in the commentary, or points made, to stimulate the readers' own thoughts on application. The question pages usually have a question on each of the sections of text that have been covered, as well as seeking to raise more general issues.

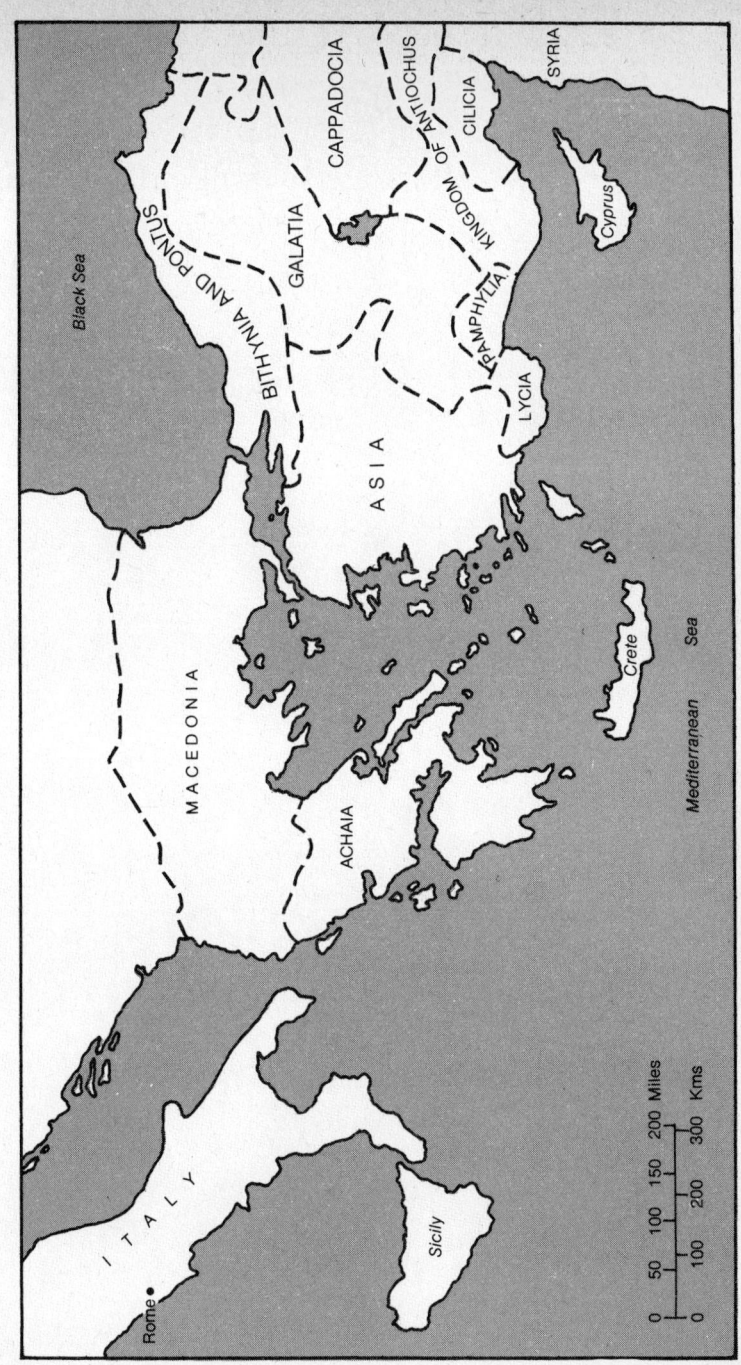

Pontus, Galatia, Cappadocia, Asia and Bithynia – the Roman provinces where Peter's first letter was circulated.

1 Peter: Contents

1:1–12 Doctrines of grace
(Part 1)

The comments on these opening verses of the epistle have been divided into two parts, as some of the most remarkable doctrines of the faith are restated in them. These concern the beginning and the end or goal of the Christian's life. God the Father is set in his rightful place as the one who is so full of mercy and grace (2,3,10) that, through the resurrection of Jesus Christ (3), he has brought about regeneration (new birth) and keeps his people for a magnificent inheritance (4,5). Not even the prophets fully understood the wonder of this message that is now revealed to Christians by the Holy Spirit (10–12). We have a privilege not even enjoyed by angels!

Verses 1–2
'Diaspora' or 'Dispersion' is a technical term for Jewish people living away from Palestine. It was first used in connection with those Israelites who were exiled throughout the ancient near-eastern world as a result of the fall of Samaria and Jerusalem. (See, for example, Isa 11:12.) It is possible that the majority of those to whom Peter writes are converted Jews. Whether or not this is so, the words 'Dispersion' and 'exiles' are probably being used metaphorically of all who find that their true home is not in this world (see 17; 2:11; Gen 23:4; Ps 39:12). The same idea of the transitory aspect of this life is found in, for example, Ephesians 2:19 and Hebrews 11:13. Peter may be building deliberately on the idea found in Paul's letters that the church is in fact the true Israel (Gal 6:16; Rom 9:6–8; Phil 3:3). This idea is developed in 2:4–12 where the Christians' identity is to be found in the fact that they are God's chosen people, and therefore they have a different home.

An emphasis on the initiating elective grace of God runs throughout this epistle but begins here in verse 2. Election, as is usual in the New Testament, is an entirely positive doctrine bringing comfort to those who otherwise, as 'strangers in the world' (NIV), would have no security. The whole Trinity is at work in this. The Spirit carries out the purposes of the Father who sanctifies (sets apart) his people for this calling, the goal of which is obedience to Jesus Christ (compare 15).

'Obedience' also introduces a prominent theme in the letter. Looking at verse 22 we see that it refers to a submissive obedience to, or acceptance of, the gospel itself. This must inevitably work itself out in relationships.

'Sprinkling with his blood' refers to the establishment of God's new covenant with his people – a covenant which brings forgiveness of sins when we have failed to obey. There is a reminder here of Exodus 24:6–8 where the covenant mediated by Moses was also ratified by blood and the people swore obedience to the Lord.

1:3–12 Doctrines of grace (Part 2)

In Greek these verses hold together as a long, carefully constructed paragraph of thanksgiving. Mercy (3) is synonymous with grace (10). Too often, as Christians become absorbed with themselves in their troubles, they forget God's graciousness. Meditating on the wonders of his grace evokes true thankfulness, whatever the circumstances, by putting God back at the centre. In concluding this section with a reference to the prophets, Peter draws attention to the fact that all of God's work of salvation in Christ was pointed to, albeit often unclearly, within the Old Testament – an argument that recalls Peter's famous speech in Acts 2. The themes so prominent here of hope, of joy before the Lord, and of an inheritance, are all apparent in the Old Testament.

The Jewish faithful had always looked with great wonder at the promise of the inheritance of the land made first to Abraham (Gen 17:8) and then again to Moses (Deut 15:4). But the land of Canaan seemed to be a thoroughly 'perishable' and 'fading' inheritance, with its occupation by foreigners and the dispersion of its people. Again the Old Testament writers foresaw something of the truth as the word 'inheritance' came to be used more widely and applied to being with the Lord himself. (See, for example, Ps 73:25–28 and 16:5–11, where the inheritance that the psalmist anticipates results in great rejoicing.)

Christ's resurrection from the dead revealed that the hope of salvation (5,9) anticipated in the Old Testament would be a future, indestructible life 'in heaven'. Even though it is secure, being 'kept' for us who are 'guarded' by God's power, yet it is *future*. It is the totality and completion of God's purposes for us. First and foremost it is a salvation from God's judgment on sinners: a salvation brought about by Christ's suffering, death and resurrection (3,11).

Peter summarizes these great truths in order to remind his readers that, as they are tested and as their vision of the inheritance fades under the pressure of their suffering, *God* remains faithful. Believing in Jesus and loving him (8) can only bring 'unutterable and exalted joy' in every situation.

Problems we may have encountered in the past with the concepts of being 'chosen' and 'kept' by God's grace can easily prevent us from appreciating them. We should let these great truths be to us what they were for Peter and the other New Testament writers – a constant source of great rejoicing and encouragement, and particularly so in the worst moments of life.

1:13–25 A proper response

'Therefore' (13) indicates the link with the preceding section. The verse provides a bridge between the discussion about God's grace and the obedience required of his children. In believing in Jesus Christians experience the great mercy of God. But there is more to come at the 'revelation' (the Second Coming) of Jesus. In view of this grace, present and future, a proper response is required. Peter turns again to the Old Testament (compare Lev 11:44–45).

Being holy does not just refer to ethical behaviour. When the Old Testament talks of God's holiness it has in mind not just his perfect goodness but his 'separateness'. In demanding that his people be holy God is showing that he has chosen them and is setting them apart for his service; their conduct, therefore, should demonstrate a total allegiance to him. This will require a strenuous effort of mind (13) and a change from former behaviour (18). 'The time of your exile' further emphasizes the *difference* between God's people and others – a point made again by the quotation from Isaiah 40:6,8 in the summary (22–25).

In great contrast to the undemanding Christianity preached today, Peter regards the 'fear' of God as motivating to good conduct. The point of v 17 is that God judges *everyone* and that includes those professing the faith. Fear of God arises from a knowledge that he is judge, from wonder at his holiness, and awe and dread that our sin required the death of Christ if it was to be forgiven. It is to this idea that Peter then turns as he discusses redemption and ransom.

Redemption, and the reference to Christ being like a lamb, recalls the passage in Isaiah 52:3 and 53:7. Again the prophets had seen something of the grace of God. But Peter is probably mixing several ideas here for, as he or any Jew thought of redemption, he would think of the Passover lamb and the exodus. Talk of 'blood' looks to the death of the victim – a death that paid a 'ransom' to take people away from their sin. Here the sacrifice for sin is linked to redemption and *payment* of a ransom to secure release from sin (Mark 10:45). This is not just a matter of deliverance from sin but of a substitutionary sacrifice made on our behalf.

If God's eternal purpose was that we should be saved in this way (20) it is no wonder that we can set our faith and hope on God with confidence. (Peter makes the same point about God's purposes in Acts 2:23.) Again the only proper response can be a total and obedient commitment to this body of truth – a commitment that will be well demonstrated in fervent love for those who hold to the same truth.

(See question 2, p 25.)

2:1–10 You are God's people

In this passage we have one of the great 'treasures' of Scripture. Now we understand better why 'love of the brethren' is so important. When a Christian is 'born anew' it is *into* a community. We call that the 'church', but interestingly, Peter does not use the word. In fact, here he is much closer to calling the community 'Israel' (see Gal 6:16), for he uses words and phrases which were applied in the Old Testament to Israel. A Christian must reflect in his life, not just the individual personal relationship with God, but the wonderful truth that he is now part of God's people. Love for the brotherhood (1:22; 2:17) is therefore a mark or badge of membership.

In verse 2 the RSV reads 'pure *spiritual* milk'. The Greek word is rare and comes from the same root as 'word' used in 1:23. So the thought of the verse is better understood as 'longing to drink the word of God'. We cannot live only on that first great experience of breathing real life; the hard work of growing up must start immediately!

As Peter writes about stones and stumbling (4–8) he uses a selection of Old Testament texts (Isa 28:16, Ps 118:22 and Isa 8:14 – note these texts also come together in Rom 9:33), adding further ideas to them. The graciousness of God continues *after* conversion. Conversion is only the first 'taste' of it (3). Christians must go on from that so that both individually and corporately as God's people they are built up into what he wants them to be: a community that belongs to God and brings honour and glory to him. Through feeding on the spiritual milk, that is through reading the word and being taught the word, we come to know Christ better and we learn how to lead lives that are 'acceptable to God through Jesus Christ' (5). We begin to see just how firm is our foundation, built on him who is our 'cornerstone' (6). Thus, not accepting the rock (Christ) is the same thing as 'disobeying the word' (8).

Reference to the 'holy priesthood' (5) anticipates v 9 where Peter spells out the privileges Christians share as part of the community. These were Israel's privileges in the Old Testament but now are possessed by the church (see Exod 19:6; Deut 7:6; Isa 43:20–21). To be a 'royal priesthood' (9) emphasizes the fact that *all* Christians are involved in the job of intercession for others and in right worship before the King of kings.

'A *holy* nation' recalls the holiness discussed in ch 1. There could be no better summary of all that Peter has said so far than the heart-warming, joyful knowledge that *'you are God's people'* (v 10; see Hos 1:6,9–10; 2:23). This is grace and mercy beyond our understanding.

What is the purpose of being granted all these privileges? It is so that 'you may declare the wonderful deeds' of God (9).

(See question 3, p 25.)

2:11–25 Exiles who suffer

Three themes noted earlier (exiles; obedience and conduct; suffering) are drawn together in this passage, as Peter begins a more specific application. Firstly, though, it is worth noting again how much Peter uses the Old Testament, and especially Isaiah. For instance, look at 22–23 and see how these verses clearly draw on Isaiah 53:9; the first part of verse 24 on Isaiah 53:12 and the second part on 53:5. Verse 25 reflects 53:6. Note also that perhaps Peter's time with Jesus may be seen in his talk of submission to the emperor (Mark 12:13–17), and his reference to Christ as Shepherd (John 10:11–16).

As 'exiles', Christians must refrain from becoming satisfied with the ways of the world through which they are passing. In the light of the verses which follow, these ways include arrogance and pride which are part of the 'passions of the flesh', referring to the inability of men and women to be submissive to each other. The Gentiles (non-Christians), need to be aware that Christians are altogether a different people. If they see this, then perhaps 'on the day of visitation' (second coming) they too will glorify God because they have come to know Christ. (It is possible that 'day of visitation' actually refers to the conversion of these people.)

Peter then moves on to give a number of areas in which Christians should 'submit' to each other, here emphasizing submission to the government and to 'masters' for whom servants (or slaves) work. It is perhaps a sign of our times that 'submission' is a much disliked term, but Peter faced this problem too! He introduces this section by saying (13), 'For the Lord's sake be submissive to every person'. (RSV: 'human institution' and NIV: 'every authority' are doubtful understandings.) If Christians are prepared to put others first, and watch after others' needs, which is the true meaning of submission, then they may suffer for doing so. Slaves may have harsh masters; wives (3:1) may have unbelieving husbands of whom they are terrified (3:6), but still a Christian life should exhibit a submission that puts others first.

The suffering referred to here (19,20) is probably not specifically persecution. In fact it is not necessarily suffering that only Christians will experience, but Christians must make sure that if they are to suffer it is for doing the right thing before the master, spouse or whoever else is concerned. The great example is Christ himself (21) who suffered 'for you'. There is, of course, no sense in which Christians suffer in order to achieve redemption, but many times in the New Testament the apostles warn that it is part of the Christian calling to suffer, like Christ, for honouring God through submission, honesty and truthfulness.

3:1–7 Husbands and wives

The biblical understanding of the relationship between men and women is, sadly, a point of great contention in the twentieth century. It is, of course, impossible to do justice to the arguments here, but we must try to do justice to the text if we are to seek to submit to Scripture. It is important not to pass over difficult texts or commands that do not seem to fit in with today's ideas. However, the context in which a letter was written, and the situation to which it was sent, cannot be ignored. It is likely that in Peter's day, as today, there were more women in the church than men, and more women with non-Christian husbands than vice versa. Given that the household was ruled by the husband it is also likely that, if a husband were converted, the wife would probably follow suit, but if a wife converted to Christ the family strains might be very considerable. Seen against this background it may be understandable why wives receive so much attention. But the relevance of this material remains!

Peter is *not* addressing wives as *inferior* to husbands. He is not talking about whether one partner is 'over' another. He assumes that men and women are 'joint heirs of the grace of life' (7). There is no question of 'status' here but, as in the previous chapter, a question of good conduct.

'Submission', we have seen, is to be a characteristic of *all* Christians to *all* people. Peter is highlighting now a foundational relationship in society: marriage. Again the motivation for this submission is to show honour to God (4,5). In the case of a non-Christian husband there is also the motivation to see him converted (1; compare 2:12).

At the heart of this passage once again is holiness (5). The examples held up from the Old Testament are women who showed that they lived differently from the world. How precisely a wife shows her calling to holiness may well vary from culture to culture: Peter is not necessarily prohibiting certain forms of dress. But the warning against defining her person in terms of her looks and sexuality is applicable today. A 'gentle' spirit requires the imitation of Christ (see Matt 11:29; 5:5). Such a woman may well be afraid of her husband's opposition, but she is precious before God and should let nothing terrify her (6).

If submission is understood biblically in terms of 'putting the other first', then the husband is actually given a very similar command when told to 'honour' his wife. Being disobedient to God in our relationships with each other will cause disharmony in our relationship with God – and our prayer life will consequently suffer (see 1 Cor 7:3–5).

3:8–17 A clear conscience

'Finally' indicates that verses 8–12 are a summary of the teaching thus far, but the ideas it contains lead Peter on to further teaching.

The summary begins with five challenges, for Christians are to be:

1. like-minded, having 'unity of spirit'. This again emphasizes the community over the individual and the need for submission to each other (see Rom 12:16).

2. sufferers together ('sympathy' RSV). The same idea is well captured by Paul when he says 'Rejoice with those who rejoice, weep with those who weep' (Rom 12:15). This draws together the themes of a separated community, with the suffering that many of them experience. When one suffers, all suffer (1 Cor 12:26).

3. loving towards fellow Christians. (See 1:22 and 2:17.)

4. tender-hearted. That is, from the very centre of their being they are to be kind to each other.

5. of 'a humble mind'. This looks back again to the example of Christ and the picture Peter has just painted of his behaviour in going to the cross and suffering for his people. It is an attitude of mind that can accept the concept of submission without trouble.

There will always be the temptation to fight back against those who cause us suffering (9). But we have been called to follow Christ; as his obedience caused him suffering (1:11), so will ours bring suffering too. Peter turns his readers to Psalm 34:11–17 as further evidence of the truth of what he is saying. (He has already quoted from Psalm 34:8 in 2:3.)

The next few verses continue to mingle the theme of suffering for what is right (14,17), with that of the need for perpetual good behaviour (16), so that people may want to know more about the gospel (15). These verses were designed to be a real encouragement to believers who might suffer to the point where they wondered whether it was all worthwhile. ('Making a defence' (15) may possibly imply a more formal persecution and the need for stating the faith in the law courts, but the passage as a whole indicates a general need to put up a defence of the faith wherever it is asked for.)

These Christians were only too well aware of 'those that do evil' (12). They were fearful and even discouraged. At the time Peter wrote, perhaps that suffering was limited to the general troubles which we have mentioned, but now he seems to look on to a time of more severe persecution. In verses 14–15 he builds on Isaiah 8:12b–13, pointing out that right and true reverence or 'fear' of the Lord will dispel fear of all else.

Calvin's comment is worth contemplating: 'How is it that we are overwhelmed with fear and think ourselves lost, when danger is impending, unless because we ascribe to mortal man more power to injure us than God to save us?'

3:18–22 Christ brings us to God

In thinking about suffering for right conduct Peter's thoughts turned to the example of Christ's suffering. But contemplation of the exemplary significance of his suffering and death always makes Peter think further about the atoning sacrifice carried through on the cross. Christ died 'once', 'for sins'. Neither he nor anyone else ever had to die in this way again. The object of this death was to pay the penalty for the sins of all who believe (1:2,18–20; 2:21,24). It was for 'our sins' (2:24, see also 1 Cor 15:3; 2 Cor 5:21), and to 'bring *us* to God' (18). This is all made so personal by Peter – but how can the discussion of the vicarious sacrifice of Christ ever be other than the most deeply personal and significant event in a Christian's life?

The expression 'put to death in the flesh but made alive in the spirit' is often misunderstood in the light of Greek dualistic thought which still affects even us in the twentieth century. Peter does not think of Christ as a 'body' on the one hand, and a resurrected 'spirit' on the other, nor does he have in mind the Holy Spirit (see NIV). Like Paul, Peter thinks in Old Testament terms of man as a unified spiritual being. It is not that flesh and body are left behind in the resurrection. The idea is, in fact, very straightforward: Christ was put to death in the sphere of the flesh (in his time as a man here on earth, see Kelly), and was made alive in the sphere of the spirit (in the place where existence is eternal and indestructible – in heaven). Thus, being made alive in such a sphere does *not* deny a true bodily resurrection (1 Cor 15:12–19).

The issues raised by these verses and 4:1–6 are exceedingly complex, and so a separate page discusses some of them. In terms of structure, verses 19–22 can be seen as a parenthesis between 18 and 4:1, and yet ideas from that parenthesis are picked up in 4:1–6. Generally, it may be noticed that the subject of 'baptism' is introduced. Peter, still comforting suffering Christians, reminds them that they committed themselves to Christ. This is witnessed to by their baptism (which has nothing to do with washing, but rather with heart-commitment) – a sign of the salvation guaranteed to them 'through the resurrection of Jesus Christ', who is now in heaven and has absolute control over all people and powers.

This is the greatest of comforts for them and for us: to know that Christ, having died for us, is at the right hand of God, and brings *us* to God.

Note: On the basis of some manuscripts verse 18 should read, 'Christ also *suffered* for sins'. This would link the thought more clearly to the preceding verses, and forward to 4:1. It would not materially alter the meaning of verse 18 itself.

(See question 7, p 25.)

Excursus: Noah and preaching to the spirits

Verse 19 indicates that, once raised from the dead, Jesus went and preached. The New Testament commentator, Kelly, usefully summarizes the exegetical questions that come to mind: **a)** who are the imprisoned spirits? **b)** what is their prison? **c)** what was proclaimed?

There are several different interpretations.

1. Some believe that this is a description of the pre-existent Christ preaching *through* Noah to those imprisoned in sin in Noah's generation.

2. Others believe that it refers to the time *between* Christ's death and resurrection, and that Christ went to the place of the dead (or to hell) where he preached to Noah's generation imprisoned there.

3. Others believe the statement concerns a proclamation to the fallen angels, who are closely linked with Noah's generation in Genesis 6:1–3 (where 'sons of God' are understood as angels), and in 2 Peter 2:4 and Jude 6. The 'preaching' may have been during the three days or during the ascension.

The problem with any interpretation that sees 'spirits' as belonging to dead people is that the word for spirits is nowhere used in this way in biblical Greek. It normally refers to either good or bad supernatural beings (eg Matt 12:45; Heb 1:14).

'Prison' is unlikely to refer to bondage to sin, as this would introduce a rather different subject from the one of encouragement and victory which is Peter's concern here. And why would Noah's generation be singled out? However, if it refers to the binding of fallen angels (see refs above and also 1 Enoch 10), then it may be a further example of Christ's total power (22) over those who break God's law and cause the people of God to suffer. However, the conclusion we come to about 'prison' will be linked to our understanding of what was 'preached'.

If the preaching referred to here is preaching the gospel to bring salvation, then two problems arise:

1. If the souls of the dead are the recipients of the proclamation then it implies there is a second chance to turn to Christ. This would be contrary to Scripture (Luke 16:25–31; Heb 9:27; 2 Cor 5:10).

2. It would be irrelevant for the fallen angels, for they are not recipients of the grace of Christ's atoning death (Heb 2:16).

However, rather than being the gracious offer of the gospel to the 'spirits', this preaching is more likely to be the straightforward proclamation (*kerusso*; compare with 4:6 where the verb translated 'preached' is *euangelizo*) of the fact that Christ is Lord, is at the right hand of God, and has all power (22).

It is certainly not possible to be dogmatic in interpreting this section of Scripture. The most generally accepted view these days, and the one which most easily fits the context of encouragement in Christ's victory over evil, is this: Christ, in his resurrected state, proclaimed his authority and power to the fallen angels.

4:1–11 Further encouragement

The problems of interpretation unfortunately do not cease in the next few verses, but Peter's intention is now clearer. As before in this epistle, the death and suffering of Christ are seen as the motivation to right conduct. In this context, Peter compares the pre-conversion behaviour of these Christians with what it should be now. In addition, he reminds them of the different gifts God has given them, as manifestations of his 'varied grace', to help them as a community to live up to their calling.

The passage begins by looking back to 3:18 where Christ's death (or suffering) for sin was mentioned. Some have suggested that Peter, in saying 'whoever has suffered . . . has ceased from sin', means that the suffering and persecution these Christians go through leads to their cleansing from sin. But elsewhere in Peter's writings and in the New Testament we know cleansing from sin comes only from *Christ's* death. Another, more likely, suggestion is that Peter is referring to a baptism liturgy – the possibility that he had a catechism or something similar in mind has already been mentioned in the Introduction. Baptism is a sign of Christ's death for us, a sign that judgment comes (3:21). Those who believe and are baptized have died with Christ, and God's verdict of the last day is already known to them: they are not regarded as sinners because they are 'in Christ' who was judged on their behalf. Romans 6:1–7 speaks similarly: verse 7 says, 'For he who has died *is* freed from sin'. Paul is referring to death *with* Christ on the cross. The challenge of baptism, and the confession of faith in Christ, is very serious and yet encouraging, especially for those who are suffering. *They know the final verdict!* What further great motivation to good conduct it now is, to know that one day you will be found 'not guilty'. Is it any wonder, then, that Christians should gladly live the lives of forgiven people, and not return to their former sinful behaviour?

Verse 6 has a number of interpretations but, in the context, the most plausible is that which keeps in mind the purpose of Peter in encouraging suffering Christians. The 'dead' are probably those in the church who have already died in these sad conditions (possibly, but unlikely, in general persecutions of Christians). These people had become Christians during their life-time when the gospel was preached to them (*euangelizo*, 4:6; compare *kerusso*, 'proclaimed', in 3:19). Thus, even though they were the recipients of unfair judgments by the world, they now live with God in the resurrection. This is further great comfort to those who die, ostracized and hated by the world for their faith.

Christ's return will bring all these sufferings to an end but, in the meantime, God's wonderful and 'varied grace' extends to providing gifts for his people to live in community together. Thus it is that, through his gifting, God enables us in all that we do to glorify him – which is our chief goal in this life (11).

4:12–19 Suffering as a Christian

The imminence of Christ's return is important in this passage (13), as it has been through the whole letter (1:5,7,13; 2:12; 4:5,7; 5:4). There is further discussion of the example of Christ and of the need to suffer for doing good rather than for wrongdoing. Verse 19 finishes the section by recalling the sovereignty of God. In these verses the pace does seem to pick up, suggesting to some that Peter is now referring to an official state persecution (see Introduction), but the intensification of the theme of suffering is better seen as a climax to Peter's argument rather than as introducing new issues.

Suffering, says Peter, is a testing and refining process for a Christian (1:6–7). There is no need to be surprised by it, because it is a necessary part of the Christian life (see Matt 5:11–12). God uses it in various ways.

1. It tests the reality of faith. If faith is not real then it will not survive testing either in terms of persecution proper or, the more normal experience, of being criticized or hated.

2. Such suffering tests the attitude of a faithful person. The Israelites were 'tested' by God through the sufferings of hunger and drought in the wilderness, but God's intention was to see the attitude of their heart, and to have them learn to rely completely on him. (See Deut 8:3.)

3. Suffering should lead to 'rejoicing'. This is a difficult concept to grasp, but it is not a false piety that Peter has in mind. Suffering shows that believers really are united with Christ. Rejoicing is not, therefore, casting a smile at the torturer nor, in fact, is it 'turning the other cheek', for these are different issues. There is no promise here that rejoicing in suffering means that a Christian suddenly no longer *feels* the pain or hurt. This is a much deeper truth. Suffering of this sort brings to the sufferers the certain knowledge that they are sharing Christ's sufferings. It is evidence of the deepest type that they truly are God's own people and redeemed by Christ. Of course, as they suffer God is with them to strengthen them in their weakness for, Peter tells them, the Spirit is with them and rests on them (14). The presence of the 'spirit of glory' is further encouragement to those who suffer for Christ as it reminds them of the way in which God was with his people in the Old Testament and protected and watched over them (see Exod 40:34–38).

The concept of judgment on the household of God can be found in Jeremiah 25:29 and Ezekiel 9:6. Peter is not suggesting that a Christian's suffering is for his own sin (that is forgiven), but that it sorts out those who are saved from those who are not. Already there is a sifting going on in the church, and if it is so serious now then just imagine the horror of the final judgment for *sin* on those 'who do not obey the gospel of God'.

What a contrast is presented! There is fearful horror in store for those who do not obey the gospel, and yet there is the present knowledge of sharing Christ's suffering and experiencing his glory for those who trust in the faithful God who sent Christ as Saviour.

5:1–14 The flock of God

The opening verses of this chapter are most poignant. Peter watched Christ suffer and ran away from the scene, but Jesus later showed him great mercy and gave him immense encouragement (John 21:15–19). Now, towards the end of his life, Peter can say with confidence that he is a 'partaker in the glory that is to be revealed'. He looks forward with great confidence, knowing that he has done what Christ has asked of him – he has fed the sheep. Now it is Peter's turn to ask the elders, the pastors and teachers of the church, to do the same.

There are two lessons to learn here because Peter is again contemplating the issue of submission – a characteristic of all true Christians. Those who are elders must lead 'eagerly' and by example, but they must not be domineering. How difficult it is to be an eager leader without being domineering! But those who are not the leaders should be humble, and accept the leadership, and listen to the word of God as it is taught. Yes, there are *roles* within the church, for not everyone is called to the same job. In fact, some are 'in charge' (2) and some not, and yet *all* are to be humble towards each other (5).

Finally, Peter sums up the message of the letter. These suffering Christians are to rely completely on God for their provision. They are to obey God and live with good conduct, knowing that Satan is alive and on the prowl. Peter ends where he began: pointing his readers to the graciousness of God. God is a 'God of all grace' (10). He has 'called' his people to a sure and eternal inheritance and he *himself* (emphatic) will look after them and care for them, strengthening them for the work of his kingdom. A doxology is surely inevitable!

This deeply moving conclusion challenges us to think over all that Peter has said. We may live in a world of trials and sufferings of all sorts, but this is where our Christianity must become practical and not just theoretical. We have a sovereign Lord who keeps us and protects us even though Satan is very much alive and prowling around. We must continue to be alert and to watch against the temptation to sin, which comes when we forget the magnitude of our salvation and the inheritance that awaits us. God is so gracious to us. What a promise on which to meditate: God 'will himself restore, establish, and strengthen' us.

Note: On Silvanus (12) and Babylon (13) see Introduction.

Questions for further study and discussion on 1 Peter

1. In what ways do you find the 'doctrines of grace' to be a comfort and support in your life?

2. Why should 'love of the brethren' be so *very* important in the context of 1:13–25? Try to work this out on the basis of chapter 1. If you get stuck then read on into chapter 2!

3. Do the privileges that you have as 'God's own people' motivate you to evangelism? Why, or why not?

4. Do you ever 'suffer' as a Christian? If the answer is 'yes', then how and why do you suffer? What effect does it have on you? If the answer is 'no', then why not? Should you expect to suffer more than you do?

5. Why is submission such a difficult subject to handle these days? In what areas ought you to submit? What is the difference between being submissive, and being servile?

6. Look at the five 'challenges' listed in the comments on 3:8–17. What do they say to you, and what may they say to the church of the twentieth century?

7. Your baptism committed you in covenantal allegiance to God; it requires you to live as a faithful Christian in the way Peter has described. Is it also a comforting sign for you?

8. What is the purpose of God's gifts (4:7–11)? Note that *two* purposes are given in these verses. Do you tend to neglect one in favour of the other?

9. What is your attitude to your 'elders' (leaders or pastors)? How can an elder lead eagerly without domineering?

2 Peter: Introduction

Recipients

2 Peter does not provide us with any indication that it was sent to a particular city or geographical area. It is probable that 3:1 is referring back to 1 Peter, in which case the destination would be the same as that given in 1 Peter 1:1. It should be noted, though, that Peter may have written other letters to other churches that we do not have.

As with 1 Peter, questions have been raised as to whether the recipients were Jews or Gentiles. Again a case can be made for a congregation made up largely of converted Jews. Reference in 3:2 to 'your apostles' points that way, and other commentators have shown possible links with the Jewish Dead Sea Scrolls. However, there are fewer allusions to the Old Testament than in 1 Peter, and no direct quotations, which may suggest a Gentile congregation.

Authorship

Most modern commentators do not accept that Peter wrote this letter. They argue that it is pseudonymous on a number of grounds:

1. There is little early witness to it as part of the canon.

2. The language and vocabulary differ considerably from that found in 1 Peter.

3. It is said that 2 Peter borrows from Jude. As an apostle of Peter's stature would not have needed to take material from another writer, Peter could not be the author. Also it is said that if 2 Peter borrowed from Jude then the apostle could not have written it as Jude was probably written after Peter's death.

4. Paul's epistles are referred to in 3:15–16 apparently as a full group of texts. Circulation of a body of Paul's letters could only have happened after Paul's death; this would mean 2 Peter was written too late to have been written by Peter.

However, none of these arguments (or others that are raised) is conclusive. In this brief Introduction a full defence of Peter's authorship – the position adopted in this commentary – is not possible, but it is offered by others such as R H Gundry, M Green and D Guthrie. Here we may make only the following points:

1. The epistle claims to be by Peter (1:1) and there are several references in the epistle which corroborate that view. See, for instance, 1:14, and the reference to the transfiguration (1:16–18).

2. Whatever the early questions raised against the canonicity of the epistle, it *was* eventually accepted as canonical. An early (third-century), and important papyrus collection of books of the New Testament (P72), shows that 2 Peter was accepted by then. But there are also possible allusions to this letter in several early second-century texts such as the *Gospel of Truth* and even *1 Clement* and *Hermas*. If Jude borrowed from 2 Peter (see below) then, of course, we would have very early (first-century) witness to the epistle.

3. The language of 1 Peter, we suggested, probably came from Peter's amanuensis, Silvanus. The apostle could well have used a different amanuensis for this letter, who would have introduced a different style and vocabulary.

4. When referring to Paul's letters, Peter did not necessarily have in mind *all* the letters of Paul we now have in the canon. For example, it is quite probable that Peter knew of 1 Thessalonians, 1 and 2 Corinthians, Galatians, Romans and some letters of which we have no record – all of which were probably written before AD 60. The fact that Peter considers these letters to be 'Scripture' is more problematic, until the whole question of apostolic authority is recalled. It is quite probable that virtually everything said and written by the apostles in the early church was regarded as having this great authority, on a par with the Old Testament. In fact Peter, if pressed, may well have understood his own writings in this light (2 Pet 1:18–21).

It would be naïve to imply that the problems associated with Petrine authorship of this letter can be dismissed in the few sentences given above, but at least we have indicated that the arguments are not all one-sided against Peter!

We assume that Peter did write it, and believe it was penned in Rome towards the end of Peter's life (early to mid-sixties AD).

Relationship to Jude
That there is a relationship between 2 Peter and Jude cannot be denied. It may be described in three ways: **a)** Peter borrowed from Jude. **b)** Jude borrowed from Peter. **c)** Both used a similar, or the same, source material.

Jude is only twenty-five verses long and fifteen of these appear in at least a very similar form in 2 Peter 2. It is impossible to be absolutely certain who borrowed from whom. However, it should be noted that if 2 Peter borrowed from Jude, there is still no need to exclude apostolic authorship of 2 Peter. We argued in 1 Peter that some form of catechism probably lay behind parts of what Peter was writing, and there is reason to suppose that he might be doing something similar here, using material that was already known as being 'anti-heretics'. The argument that a great apostle would not draw on a minor figure like Jude is a non-starter. Firstly, Jude was also regarded as having apostolic authority (see Introduction to Jude), and secondly, as Gundry says, 'Literary history is full of examples of prominent writers who borrowed from obscure sources. (Shakespeare is one who did).'

Suggestions that Jude drew on 2 Peter are made on several grounds:

1. Peter often talks about the false teachers in the future tense, while Jude views them as already present. Some even suggest that Jude 17–18 looks back to 2 Peter 3:2,3. But Peter does not always use the future tense of these heretics.

2. Jude is more polished in its structure than is 2 Peter, and this may indicate a careful and reflective re-working of Peter's material. However, it may also mean that Peter simply remembered Jude's work and re-wrote it in a more relaxed way.

3. It is also often asked why Jude would have bothered to re-write 2 Peter in such a very short letter, while adding a minimum of his own ideas. However, he does tell us that he writes with a certain urgency

(Jude 3) and 'to remind you' (5). So perhaps he found Peter's letter to be the most useful message to pass on (again?) to the congregation.

Purpose and teaching

Peter was writing to a church or churches – paralleled by many today – where false teaching was on the increase. He warned against teachings that denied the return of Christ, and that allowed a weakening in moral conduct.

The fact that Christ had not returned was apparently of some concern to the early Christians, and so this was an area where a careful and concerted attack by false teachers might gain them some reward. Peter, however, puts an entirely different perspective on the apparent delay in Christ's return. He sees the 'day of the Lord' coming in a similar way to that described in the Gospels: 'like a thief' – unexpectedly (3:10, see Matt 24:43). Meanwhile, there is a period of great grace for, although judgment is deserved, the Lord holds back in order that people should repent of their sins. The subject of the judgment to come is important, because, says Peter, those very people who deny it must learn that *they* will be judged.

In fact, as Christians await that great day they must 'be zealous' about doing what is right, in order to be found ready for the Lord on his return. Thus Peter's stress on the second coming is also the stick he uses to admonish the heretics over their false teaching on morality.

Outline

Chapter 1 begins with the basic message of which Peter wishes to remind the congregation. The purpose of this reminder is given in verses 11 and 12. As Peter nears the end of his life he wishes, again, to insist on the absolute truth of the message that has been proclaimed.

Chapter 2 warns against the rise of false teachers, and uses allusions to the Old Testament to show that they will be judged for their various sins.

Chapter 3 draws attention to the effect that 'scoffers' and others will have among these Christians, but God's word and his promises are utterly to be trusted. Christ will return and judge the people; meanwhile there is work to be done!

2 Peter: Contents

1:1–15 A reminder

Peter's introduction (1–2) is interesting. First, after establishing his apostolic credentials, he talks of his audience as those who have an 'equal standing'. It is a common failing of Christians in all generations to think of themselves as something less than other Christians, or as having less by way of privilege. The comparison Peter makes here, nearing the end of his life (13–15), is between himself, as one of the privileged generation of eyewitnesses, and subsequent generations who have not 'seen' in this way. The basis of the equal privilege, shared by Peter and others, is that God himself is just ('righteousness' used as an ethical quality – see 2:5,7; 3:13 etc). In other words, God is utterly fair in granting to all those who have faith, the *same* privileges. (This may remind us of an occasion when Peter drew attention to the *same* faith among different people: Acts 11:17.) This thought is really worth meditating upon. We have equal privileges with Peter!

Secondly, it is worth noting Peter's phrase 'our God and Saviour Jesus Christ'. There is much debate these days about whether Christ is actually called 'God' in the Bible. While some see this as a reference to *two* persons ('our God and the Saviour Jesus Christ'), most agree that the Greek links Christ to God explicitly, thereby calling Christ God. The term 'Saviour', used of Jesus less than twenty times in the New Testament, was regularly used of God himself in the Old Testament. Jesus, who is God, carried out God's own plan for the saving of his people.

'The knowledge of God' (2, also 3,8; 2:20) is fundamental if false teachers are to be confronted properly. That is what Peter wants his readers to remember – all that they have previously learned from the apostles and Scripture. This is the truth in which they must be established (12). It is the knowledge of who Christ is (3), of the promises made to those of faith (4), of the need for a proper response of faith, obedience and growth in Christian life (4–8). It is the knowledge that each Christian must seek to live a life that confirms his or her call from God, and above all it is the knowledge of an eternal kingdom ruled by the Lord Christ (11).

It is a sad comment on the church today that 'knowledge' and teaching receive so little attention. The emphasis is rather on 'experience'. 'How do I *feel* about Jesus today?' is more likely to be asked than 'What more do I *know* about Jesus today?' This is a sad dichotomy, and a wrong one. We must experience the presence of Christ in our lives daily. We must grow in our love for him, but also in our *knowledge* of him. Only if we do this will we be able to recognize and deal with the false teachers in our churches, who often *claim* to have the same 'experience' as true Christians.

1:16–21 Witnesses to the truth

In this passage it becomes clear that Peter feels he has to defend his account of the gospel. Exactly what sort of false teaching he was up against is unclear, but the general problem of false teaching was already present in the church and not only to be expected in the future (2:1). The main problem Peter addresses here seems to be that of the reliability of the teaching that Christ will return.

1. The apostolic witness

Note that Peter starts with a change from 'I' to 'we'. He shows that this message is the one not just he, but all the apostles, had made known. 'Eyewitnesses' probably refers to all the apostles, although the example of the transfiguration which he gives (17–18) only included Peter, James and John (Matt 17:1–8).

Presumably some people had been saying that what the apostles were teaching were 'cleverly devised myths'. The word 'myth' meant a variety of things in Greek just as it does in English today. In the light of the description 'cleverly devised' we assume it refers to *untrue* stories or fables. Greek philosophers and writers held such fables in contempt. There was particular disdain for myths to do with prophecy and the next world and, from the context, it may be that it was on this subject of the future coming of Jesus that Peter was receiving the greatest challenge.

The word 'coming' (16, *parousia*) usually denotes the second coming (3:4,12). Peter refers to 'the power and coming of our Lord Jesus Christ', and confirms that it is *not* a myth because he and other disciples have already witnessed Jesus' 'majesty'. He gives the example of the transfiguration as evidence that Christ will come again. The importance of this example is twofold: **a)** it revealed Christ in 'majesty' and 'glory' (both words often used of God himself: Luke 9:43; 2 Cor 4:6,15 etc); **b)** it included the confirmation by the Father of who Jesus is. Peter probably saw the reference to 'my Son' as fulfilment of Psalm 2:6,7 where the 'holy mountain' is also mentioned. In other words, the transfiguration showed Jesus to be the King 'set . . . on Zion, my holy hill' (Ps 2:6). Since, then, the King would come, the transfiguration experience had borne witness to Peter that the King would be none other than Jesus.

2. The witness of Old Testament prophecy

This is why Peter, secondly, insists that Old Testament prophecy is also a true witness to the future coming of Christ (19–21). Time and again the apostles showed that their message was true because it had been foretold in Scripture – the unbreakable word of God. The Scriptures are the light revealing the depths of God's plan and purposes for his people now and in the future, until Christ himself comes. They come directly from God himself (21).

Belief in the utter truth of Scripture confirms faith and gives the believer boldness in the battle against false teaching.

2:1–22 Judgment on false teachers

This passage is painful, even depressing, to read. It deals with a subject as relevant today as ever it has been. But it is a subject of which little is heard in the twentieth century: judgment. False prophets were judged (1a) and false teachers will be judged (1b). Just as the Old Testament bears true witness to the second coming of Christ, so it bears witness to the horror of judgment wrought on such people by God Almighty. The illustrations Peter uses are serious when considered individually, but here, in his grouping of them (possibly using Jude or an early church list of judgments), they are worse.

The picture Peter paints with such bold brush strokes is like one of those great Victorian paintings of a violently wind-swept hillside with grey clouds that seem greyer and larger than life. The sense of desolation, of anger and of lostness pervades the scene. The tragedy here is that this is not larger than life, this is not Victorian romanticism, this is real life in which real judgment takes place.

Individual incidents are examined in a little more detail when we look at Jude; here it is best to read the whole chapter quite rapidly to get the overall feeling of horror Peter conveys. Note the *inevitability of the judgment* that cannot be escaped: 'their condemnation has not been idle' (3); 'to be kept' (4); 'turning . . . to ashes' (6); 'to keep the unrighteous under punishment . . .' (9); 'and especially . . .' (10); 'will be destroyed' (12) etc.

Note also the *totality and type of judgment*: 'destruction' (3); 'into hell' (4); 'to extinction (destruction)' (6); 'suffering wrong for their wrongdoing' (13 – not that God does them wrong, but that they receive a punishment consistent with the harm they have done). Yet, there is more, for as certainly as there is judgment, so there is *deliverance for the righteous*. This is not a dominant theme in the chapter, but comes through in verses 5,7a,9a.

Sometimes it seems that Christians expect false teachers to wear a placard around their necks saying who they are! Here the false teachings were brought in 'secretly'. It is important to see that the danger is far greater than is often realized. They 'deny the Master' (1) by being licentious (2) and not obeying the Lord who owns them.

It is easy to see how others are led astray, but it is an uncomfortable and necessary task to look at ourselves and our own teachers to see if we, too, remain unaware of the subtleties of the enemy. Finally, the greatest and saddest irony is that those who deny the future judgment are the very ones for whom it is reserved.

3:1–9 A time of grace

Recalling the two witnesses of chapter 1, Peter desires that the congregation should remember (1:13) the predictions of the prophets and the word of the Lord received through the apostles. The truth was known, but they needed to be reminded to hold to it in the face of 'scoffers' (3).

These people will come 'in the last days'. The 'last days' can be future, but usually refer to the whole time between Christ's first and second coming. The apostles thought of themselves as living in this period of history, just as we should (1 Pet 1:20; Heb 1:2). The irony we noted in chapter 2 continues here: that people scoff at the prospect of a future coming (4) is in fact evidence that Christ will come!

Peter looks forward to a time that had already begun, when first generation Christians (fathers) had died and Christ had still not come. This verse need not indicate a late date for the writing of the letter (that is, when the first generation had already died). Peter was about to die, and had seen some of his generation die and be martyred. This was a crucial time for the early church. They had to learn to come to terms with the eyewitness dying *before* Christ's second coming (see 1 Thess 4:13–18).

In the light of statements today by some churchmen that God does not work miraculously in history, it is interesting to note that the problem of rationalism was already present in Peter's day. False teachers taunted Christians with the view that 'all things always carry on in the same way'. Those rationalist teachers who claim to be so 'modern' in their approach to religion might do well to take note of Peter's answers!

Peter makes three points here.

1. To the scoffers he points out that God's word is the basis on which everything continues to happen and, anyway, that word has clearly been seen to work in strange and 'abnormal' ways (6) which will be seen again at the judgment (7). Of course, they would not be persuaded by these arguments unless the Lord opened their eyes to the truth. But Peter's main concern here is to build up and encourage believers.

2. So he comforts Christians by recalling Psalm 90:4. What may seem a long wait to them, is, in God's eyes, a short period. 'Time is God's gift, and he has bidden us to watch, pray and work' (Green, p 134).

3. But it is the third point which is so fascinating. Peter points to the delay as being evidence that we live in a time of grace . . . there is still time for repentance (see Ezek 18:32)!

Note: The reference to 1000 years is a figure of speech. Peter is *not* saying that in the Bible 1000 years should be substituted whenever we read 'day'!

3:10–18 The coming day of God

Even though the delay in Christ's coming reveals God's grace, yet the day will most certainly come unexpectedly (10, see Luke 12:39–40). It is therefore necessary to consider the sort of people we should be in these 'last days' while we wait (12) for 'the day'. The idea of the 'day of God' comes from the Old Testament and refers to God's judgment (7; see, for example, Isa 13:9). One response to the delay in judgment is to go the way of the false teachers: into immorality. Verse 10 shows what folly this would be.

The imagery Peter uses to describe that day is vivid and drawn largely from other scriptures (eg Ps 18:12–15; Isa 34:4; Joel 3:15–16a). The picture is of a great cosmic tragedy involving fire. Some have suggested that this will be seen in nuclear war. This cannot be known, but the spectre of nuclear war gives an awe-inspiring picture of the terror which that 'day' will hold for non-believers. But many Christians today have a most unbiblical fear of such conflagration! Christians are awaiting a new heaven and a new earth (13), and *if* the Lord should choose to show his power and exercise his judgment in nuclear war (which we pray he will not), still they should remember that he 'will be a refuge for his people' (Joel 3:16b), and that Christ will be coming in that 'day' for his people, to fulfil his promises to them. The judgment day for Christians is not summarized in the despairing cry, 'It's the end of the world', but in a glorious cry, 'Our Lord has come – it's the beginning of a new earth in which righteousness dwells'.

Peter encourages his readers (11,14) to lead lives of holiness and godliness and to be 'at peace' – that is at peace with God (Rom 5:1). Surprisingly, they are to 'hasten the coming' (12). There is a close relationship between repentance and the coming of the Lord (8–9), and perhaps Peter has in mind here an idea developed further in later Jewish thought (see Bauckham, p 312), that the Lord's coming may be hastened in the light of man's repentance (compare the ideas of Isa 59:20 and Acts 3:19).

The gospel was distorted early on. Apparently false teachers attacked some of the deeper areas of Pauline theology that even Peter admits are not easy to understand! There is a candid honesty here, but Peter's main point is that the Scriptures, which include some of Paul's writings, all say the same as Peter himself has been saying.

The great glory of this letter, for its first recipients and for us, is here in the last two verses. Because we have been warned we can beware of error, and we can do better what we should: 'Grow in the grace and *knowledge* of our Lord'.

Note: 'Burned up' (10) probably means 'be disclosed'. That is, God's fiery wrath and judgment will find out and destroy all that is evil.

Questions for further study and discussion on 2 Peter

1. What are the 'equal privileges' that Christians share with Peter and the apostles?
What difference ought this teaching to make in your life?

2. Knowledge of God and experience of a relationship with God need to be carefully balanced in the Christian life. 'Experience' may simply be wrong, and knowledge without a personal love and experience of God is no use to anyone. Does the balance in your life or in your church weigh towards one rather than the other?
What should be done to restore a biblical balance?

3. Would you find it easy to recognize a false teacher?
How would you recognize one?

4. Do you look forward longingly for the return of Christ?
What difference does it make to the way you live if you know that while Christ's return is delayed there remains more time for grace?

5. Are you afraid of the dangers of the age in which we live (nuclear war, for instance)? How should our confident hope for the future and our belief in the coming 'day' of the Lord relate to these fears?

The letters of John: Introduction

The background situation that gave rise to these letters has long been debated, as have questions of dating and authorship. In reality it is almost impossible to avoid some speculation on these issues as we seek to understand the part of New Testament Christianity known as Johannine theology. As these letters are read, it becomes obvious that they contribute to our theology in important areas which are either not addressed, or are dealt with in a different manner, by other New Testament writers.

Authorship

Although it is clear that the author was well known by those to whom he wrote (1 John 2:1), he never actually says who he is (a point of similarity with the Gospel of John). In 2 and 3 John he calls himself the 'elder'. There is a strong tradition from early times that the apostle John was the author and certainly the disciples could be referred to as 'elders'. However, some have suggested, on the basis of an ambiguous statement by Papias (Bishop of Hierapolis, c AD 130), that two 'Johns' were known: the apostle, and a still living 'elder' called John. On the other hand, Guthrie points out (pp 864–865) that the letters were accepted as canonical by the church fathers on grounds that included apostolic authorship, and it is unlikely that they would have been confused about two people called John. What evidence there is probably balances more in favour of the traditional view that the apostle John was the author of the letters.

The recipients

As with 1 and 2 Peter, it seems that the recipients of 1 John were probably a mixture of converted Jews and Gentiles. 5:21 may suggest a Gentile audience, if it is assumed that Jews did not have a problem with idols. But 'idols' may have a much broader significance referring to the generality of pagan ideas involved in the false teaching known to the church. As we shall see in the commentary, many of the theological ideas John draws upon have their background in the Old Testament. Recent scholarly work has also shown links between some of the ideas seen in the Jewish Dead Sea Scrolls (largely written in the first century BC) and those in the Johannine literature. While these similarities are sufficient to emphasize the Jewishness of many of John's ideas, John's theology is, of course, utterly Christian, and so parts company with the thought reflected in the Dead Sea Scrolls, particularly where it concerns the *way* in which salvation comes about.

It is also worth making the point that just because John, or any other New Testament writer, is deeply indebted to Jewish thought and background, it does not *necessarily* indicate that his audience were converted Jews. We easily forget, these days, that all basic teaching that new converts received centred on the sayings of the Lord and apostles *and* on the exposition and interpretation of the Old Testament.

Probably John was writing to a group of churches that he knew well in the province of Asia. The apostle John was linked by early Christian writers with the large town of Ephesus and, if he also wrote Revelation, then the towns surrounding Ephesus may have been the recipients of these letters too (see the letters of Rev 2–3).

The 'elect lady and her children' who are the recipients of 2 John are probably one of those churches in Asia. Whether the 'elect lady' was a personal acquaintance of the apostle, or a title that he gives to the church as a whole is disputed.

3 John, on the other hand, is more clearly personal in its address. The letter is sent to Gaius and it rebukes Diotrephes by name and, also by name, praises Demetrius. The same general area around Ephesus is probably where these people lived.

Purpose and teaching

1 John

John writes this apparently general letter to encourage followship and joy in the church (1:3–4) and to help them to be certain of their faith (5:13–14). But he finds it necessary to do this because of the false teaching entering the church.

It is difficult to be certain what the false teachers were propounding. Some have suggested it was a heresy known as gnosticism that came to the fore in the second century under teachers like Marcion. This heresy had many forms but it was essentially dualistic, separating matter and flesh (regarded as evil) from the spirit (regarded as good). Interestingly, this had two almost opposite results in its adherents: a) some became totally immoral because they believed bodily matters (eg sexual behaviour) were unimportant. Only the spiritual area of one's life was important so a person could do anything with the body and not affect the spiritual realm of existence. b) Others became ascetics. Because bodies were part of evil matter, they were determined to suppress bodily desires at all costs.

The word 'gnosticism' comes from the Greek word 'knowledge' – through the possession of secret knowledge the immortal spirit might reach heaven. Gnosticism gradually became quite influential in the Roman Empire and developed all sorts of rather strange and elaborate systems by which the spirit could rise above the material realm to the spiritual world. Essentially it was syncretistic as a religion, drawing on many different religious ideas. It is thus not surprising that it made inroads into Christianity. The problem is that while basically Greek dualistic ideas were clearly present in the first century AD (as they had been since Plato's time and before), there is little evidence that gnosticism itself developed before the second century. Perhaps the false teachers John confronted had some of the characteristics of these later heretics, but it is doubtful that this had yet become their religion.

As we read 1 John we find that John emphasizes certain key themes and we therefore may be right in assuming that the false teachers were especially wrong in these particular areas of their theology. Two obvious matters that John discusses in this letter are **1.** Christology (Who is Christ?) and **2.** ethics (How are Christians to behave?).

1. *Christology.* John emphasized that he had actually *seen* Christ and the events that gave rise to the gospel message (1:1–4). He stressed that Jesus is the Son of God (1:3; 2:22; 5:5,11). He reminded his readers of Jesus' pre-existence (2:13–14), and of his second coming (2:28). Jesus is righteous and perfect (2:29), and has come as a human in the flesh (4:2, see 2:6; 4:17). He is the Saviour who loves his people and has taken away sin (4:10,14). Perhaps, therefore, false teachers had challenged whether Jesus was truly human, arguing that he only seemed to be so. The human Jesus is shown by John to be both God and man. Smalley (pp xxiii–xxvi) suggests that John faced two problem groups, one ex-pagan, over-emphasizing the divinity of Christ, and one ex-Jewish, over-emphasizing the humanity of Christ. Against both, he says, John 'provides a balanced Christology'. It is difficult to agree that there is enough evidence to suggest a two-fronted opposition. But it is worth watching the undoubted 'balance' in the discussion of who Christ is as these letters are read.

2.) *Ethics.* If Jesus is all this then how should his church behave? As he is righteous and perfect and has cleansed us from sin, Christians should be righteous in the way they live (1:6–2:6,15–17; 3:4–10 etc). As he first loved them, so they should love (4:19; 2:7–11; 3:14–18; 4:20–21 etc). Perhaps some of the false teachers had begun to exclude others from their 'in'-group, thinking of themselves as perfect and better than others. John reminds them that they are not perfect (1:8–10) and they must love all Christians.

2 John
In this letter similar themes are present, with great emphasis on truth (against false teachers) and love among Christians.

3 John
This differs somewhat from 1 and 2 John, looking at what seems to be an ecclesiastical dispute. But the stress on 'the truth' is still dominant (3–4,12), and lack of love is mentioned in the work of Diotrephes (9–10).

Date
The dating of these letters is difficult. Being written by the apostle or by another 'eyewitness' means that they cannot really be dated much after AD 90. In that they seem to reflect, in various ways, work later than John's Gospel, then the dating of the letters is also tied up with the dating of the Gospel. Recently J A T Robinson has reminded us of just how difficult these issues are by suggesting that the Gospel was written decades earlier than most scholars believe, appearing in its 'first edition' as early as AD 50–55, and the letters a decade later. (See J A T Robinson, *The Priority of John.* London: SCM, 1985.) Most of those who accept apostolic authorship of the letters (as we do here) have suggested dates between AD 70 and 90.

Outline: 1 John
Chapter 1 A preface establishes the truth of John's testimony and his purpose in writing (1–4). This leads into a discussion concerning the behaviour of those who have fellowship with God.

Chapter 2 Christians should be obedient to the Lord (3–11), know the Father and love him rather than the world (12–17). The danger is that Satan is at work and they must beware of antichrists – those who deny that Jesus is the Messiah and deny the Father and the Son (22).

Chapter 3 God is righteous, so Christians should do right and be seen to be God's children (1–10). In particular, Christians should love each other (11–24).

Chapter 4 Again, though, the real and evident danger of false teaching must be taken seriously and Christians must not become 'worldly' – limited in their thinking by sinful human values (1–6). They must love each other because God is love (7–21).

Chapter 5 Belief in and love for God reveal true Christians; for such people obedience to God is not burdensome (1–5). The content of true Christianity should be clear (6–12). A conclusion summarizes what has been said.

1, 2 and 3 John: Contents

1:1–10 The message proclaimed

The first four verses are complicated. The main verb in the sentence is 'we proclaim' (3), but here John is drawing attention to the substance of the message proclaimed. It concerns the 'word of life' (1), which refers probably both to the person of Jesus and to the message itself that John proclaims about God and his Son.

John emphasizes that this 'was from the beginning'. It had been God's plan from before the foundation of the earth to send Jesus, and Jesus, who had existed with God back in eternity (who is eternal life – 2), has now come to earth. This is the message and the person that is proclaimed. John further tells us that Jesus has been witnessed – touched, heard and seen. In a day and age when even theologians can doubt the truth of the incarnation of Jesus, John's message speaks clearly. He proclaims what he *saw* and *heard* (3). It is likely that John was beginning his letter with a full-blown attack on some of the false teachers who denied that Jesus had really come in the flesh, perhaps insisting that he only seemed to be human but was really just a spiritual being.

The purpose of this proclamation (3,4) was that the recipients should have fellowship like John with the Father and Jesus, and that John's joy may be complete. 'Fellowship' is a word that is much too glibly used these days. Usually we take it simply to refer to 'enjoying things together'. But the fact that it is 'with the Father...', and in the light of the way it is expanded later (6), clearly shows that it involves much more. It is ultimately union with God through having faith in the Son. This will lead us to enjoy friendship with each other and to sharing things, but John's purpose is that we should be one in Christ by believing in the word of life which he and the other apostles are proclaiming. This becomes clearer (7) when fellowship with one another is linked to walking in the light and to being cleansed from sin. Fellowship is not just having a cup of coffee together, but it is belonging to God by believing in the Son of God (6–7; 5:13), enjoying that faith together and sharing together in its privileges and gifts. (See question 1, p 56.)

Verses 5–10 re-emphasize the nature of this message. Fellowship with God (6) and with each other (7) involves living out the truth of our faith. We cannot 'walk in darkness' (6), and we must not claim to be sinless (8). Sadly, these verses are all too relevant today as well. Some still claim that once they belong to the Lord they are no longer likely to sin. To suggest this is to make God a liar (10). Others still continue in sin forgetting that their fellowship is supposed to be with God who can tolerate no darkness at all (5). What joy it is that we as sinners receive cleansing and forgiveness from our sin because Jesus died for us (7,9).

2:1–6 Sins forgiven

Having introduced us to the need to admit our sin and to the faithfulness of God in forgiving us (1:7–9), John now expands his message. In spite of the fact that he recognizes that all Christians will sin, one of John's purposes in writing is that we should not do so (1). In this John remains faithful to the whole biblical message (7). God is light and is not present by his Spirit in those who do evil and who follow the self-centred ideals of the world, that is, who are proud and covetous and love those things that the world can give them more than they love God (15–17). Christians must understand this. God demands righteousness. But it is no good saying that we are righteous when in fact it is clear that no human being has ever been wholly so. The only human who has ever been correctly called 'the righteous' is Christ (1).

John urges us not to sin, but he knows the limitations of men and women, and knows himself, so he thanks God that when we do sin all is not lost for we have an advocate (lawyer) who will plead our cause with the Father. Jesus does this on the basis of his own righteousness, and the sacrifice that he has made for our sins. The RSV talks of 'expiation', other versions use 'propitiation' or 'atoning sacrifice'. 'Expiation' refers to the fact that sin is dealt with or covered. 'Propitiation' has in mind a God who is justly angry with sin and who demands a sacrifice to placate that wrath. 'Atoning sacrifice' (NIV) seems to include both ideas in that the sacrifice is obviously offered to God, and the word 'atoning' involves the idea of something being done to deal with sin. The context seems to stress 'propitiation' as Christ has offered himself as a sacrifice for our sins (1:7) and is now pleading before God himself on our behalf. The same idea is present in 4:10.

'For the sins of the whole world' (2) does not imply that all people will be saved but that Christ's death is an atoning sacrifice for people all over the world who 'know God', whatever their nationality or race.

The concept of 'knowing God' here, as elsewhere in the Bible, is virtually the same thing as having fellowship with him. It is more than simply having theoretical understanding for it involves obedience to, and full love for, the Lord. Again we must not deliberately continue to sin and yet claim to have knowledge of God (3–6). For us one of the evidences of our Christian faith will be that we desire to keep God's commandments. If we keep God's words (5) then 'God's love' (not 'love for God' – RSV) is seen to be complete in our lives (see 4:7). Our assurance that we are God's own children lies both in the fact that God loved us and sent his Son to die for us so that our sins could be forgiven, and also in the fact that as we keep God's commandments we actually see his love at work in our lives helping us.

(See question 2, p 56.)

2:7–17 The true light already shines

Note the gentle pastoral concern that John shows for those to whom he is writing: 'My little children' (1), 'Beloved' (7), 'little children' (12), 'children' (18) etc. In these verses he moves on from a discussion of 'knowing God' and the need for obedience (4–5), to the issue of claiming to live in the light and the consequent need to love the brotherhood of believers (9–10). Even in the way he writes John is offering an example of the way that love may be expressed.

No doubt John has in mind John 13:34 at this point. There Jesus talks of giving a new commandment that his disciples should love one another. The links with what he has said before (1:5–7) are obvious. The law to love and to 'walk in the light' was, of course, not new. It formed the basis of the Old Testament law (Lev 19:18,34; Deut 6:5; Isa 2:5). John stresses this fact against those who would perhaps have said, as some do today, that behaviour is not particularly important once one is a Christian. But he also probably has in mind people who were saying that this Christianity, with its emphasis on love, was some new sort of religion. How often these days people try to drive a wedge between the one they call the 'God of the Old Testament' and the 'God of love of the New Testament'! God is the same yesterday, today and for ever. Moral behaviour, as laid down by God in the Old Testament, is still important.

However, in another sense this *is* a new commandment, for it is now 'true in him' (8), that is, it is seen in Christ himself. Jesus has shown what God's love really is, in giving himself for us (4:8–12). We therefore have an example to follow. Further, we now live in a situation in which the true light is already shining (8). Because the 'last days' have come and Jesus is now exalted, awaiting his return in glory at his second coming, we know that darkness is passing. Even love among Christians reflects the fact that the light of God and of his Son is already shining in this world.

The practical implications of this are now laid out. We are to love each other, and this is addressed to all members of the community. Love is an important characteristic of a Christian. Without it, there is only darkness – no reflection of the character of God (9,11,15). Notice that he refers to 'little children' (12; probably meaning everyone), 'fathers' (13; probably meaning the spiritual leaders in the church who are responsible for the others) and 'young men' (13–14; probably those young people who are going through an age of particular temptation).

John emphasizes God as 'Father' here. We must obey him, love him and do his will (17). But we also know the Father (13), and our sins are forgiven by him (12). Therefore we must continue to let his word rule our lives (14).

(See question 3, p 56.)

2:18–27 The dangers of heresies

These verses continue to draw out sharply the differences between heretics and Christians. Heretics split themselves off from the church (19), deny that Jesus is the Christ (the Messiah – 22) and deceive people (26), whereas Christians have been anointed with the Spirit of Christ and know the truth (20–21), confess the Son (23) and do not waver in their commitment to the truth (24,27).

For the meaning of the 'last hour' see on 2 Peter 3:1–9 where 'last days' means the same thing. A sign that we are in this period of time is that 'antichrists' have come. These are people who deliberately set themselves against Christ, even denying that Jesus is the Messiah. There has been a lot of speculation as to whether there is to be one particular 'antichrist' as well as these 'antichrists' (18), and whether the antichrist is a person or a principle of evil present in those who seek to deny basic elements of the gospel message. The word 'antichrist' appears only in John's letters (but also see 2 Thess 2:1–12 for a similar idea).

In the light of 4:3, where it is the 'spirit of antichrist' that is mentioned, it is possibly correct to say that John has in mind a principle of evil which is manifested in certain people. These would be those who speak against Christ in some way. This view is supported by 2:22 where 'the antichrist' refers generally to those who deny Jesus as the Messiah. Whether John was looking for a *particular* antichrist at the end of time embodying all that is evil is not clear from this verse. John's point – especially relevant in this age – is that there *are* antichrists around and that they attack the church. We must recognize that their special area of attack will be the person of Jesus for they will try to persuade us that he is not who the Bible tells us he is: the Messiah and the Son of God. It is exceedingly easy to be deceived by such people today just as it was back in John's day. Some will even argue against Jesus' divinity or his pre-existence in order, they say, to make the gospel more relevant and meaningful to the twentieth century!

The way of counteracting false teaching is to understand and live according to the apostolic teaching which has been learned (24; letting it 'abide in you'), and to rely upon the Holy Spirit who will teach the truth (20,27). The talk of 'anointing' in these verses refers to the work of the Holy Spirit who confirms the truth of the word of God in our hearts (3:24; 4:13; 5:7; see 2 Cor 1:21–22). This does not mean that we no longer have any need for teaching, as some in our churches suggest today. Rather the opposite is true. We need proper teaching of the whole gospel of Christ, and the Holy Spirit will lead those who are true Christians (those who persevere – 'continue' – 19) to recognize that which is true and that which is a lie.

(See question 4, p 56.)

2:28–3:10 No one born of God sins

In summary, people should keep themselves safe from the antichrists by 'abiding in him' (28). As we have already seen, abiding in Christ involves complete commitment to him in relying upon his promises (25), in learning more about him and holding fast to the original teaching received on becoming a Christian (24). But remaining in Christ is vital for another reason: 'so that when he appears we may have confidence'.

Having 'confidence' and not being 'shamed' refers to the Christian's standing before the judgment seat when Christ comes. Is it not arrogant to talk of having confidence before God? Yet that is just what we can have because we are God's children (3:2) and because we are relying on *God*'s promises, not on our own works. This is the direct and great manifestation of the love of God for us (3:1). The wonderful fact is that 'abiding' in Christ means that we can have absolute confidence for the future because *God* keeps his promises.

Two words are used here of Christ's second coming: 'revealed' ('appears', 28a) and 'parousia' ('coming', 28b). The first word refers to the revealing of what is at present not seen. The second is a common word for the second coming. It introduces us to the subject that will be raised in 3:2 where John confirms that there is a future for those who are now God's children, but that that future is integrally bound up with the coming of Jesus. Then, and only then, will the nature of our future be 'revealed'.

In verse 29 John is not saying that if we do right things we shall be saved. This verse continues to build the confidence of Christians: children of God can do what is right precisely because they are God's family. If you, as a Christian, do what is right, it is a further indication for you that you really are a child of God. Of course, this does not mean that everyone who does a few right things is 'born of God' (see 3:23).

A similar point is made in 3:3. The one whose hopes are bound up in Christ has recognized the purity of Christ and so seeks to be Christ-like even now in this life.

The challenge of this passage of Scripture can easily be ignored. It seems too radical and impossible. It almost seems that Christians should be perfect! (See next page.) The point is this: sin is a characteristic of a child of Satan, while godliness and purity are to be characteristics of children of God. Again and again John has emphasized the incongruity of sin in the life of a believer. False teachers may suggest that behaviour does not really matter (7), but it does. Christians have a new nature (9) and they should live according to that nature.

Excursus: Sinless Christians?

The challenge of 2:28–3:10 is so strong that some have suggested that John is here teaching that all Christians can and should be perfect. Through history a number of Christian groups have argued just this, and some today still point to these verses as evidence that a real Christian never sins. After all, they say, John is quite clear: 'No one who abides in him sins; no one who sins has either seen him or known him' (3:6).

There are two immediate problems with this view of the section:

1. It is the clear experience of Christians that they continue, throughout their lives, to be in need of the forgiveness of God. After all, sin is much more than a direct transgression of God's law in a given day. As the Westminster Shorter Catechism puts it: 'Sin is any *want of conformity unto*, or transgression of, the law of God'.

2. John himself would then seem to be inconsistent. In 1:8–10 he was very careful to show that it was the *false* teachers who taught perfectionism. 'If we say we have not sinned, we make [God] a liar and his word is not in us'. This assumes that Christians are sinners, for they are the ones who have God's word in them.

Various explanations have been given of what John really means:

1. It is pointed out by some that this passage is talking of 'abiding' or 'remaining' in Christ. The opposite is 'abiding' or 'remaining' in sin. Thus, it is said, that John is speaking not against people whose sins occur on an occasional basis and for which there is an advocate (2:1), but against those who continue to live in sin with no attempt to change. This view may be supported by the use of the present tense in these verses which can be continuous in Greek: 'No one who continues to sin . . .' (NIV – 6,9).

2. Another way of understanding this section is to realize that it begins with a discussion of the second coming. John is looking at the total relationship of the believer with the Father. For the present an ideal is stated: that Christians do not sin. Our future is certain: eternity with the Lord (2:24–25). We are confident of the judgment day because we are 'in Christ' who is righteous (2:28–29; 3:2–6), therefore we too are to be judged righteous. Before we are perfected at Christ's coming, we must therefore learn to be in practice what we know we are and know we shall be 'in Christ'. The ideal is before us. However, even as believers who know it is 'unchristian' to sin, we need to be exhorted to good conduct again and again and to recognize that we still need our Advocate.

In conclusion, it must be said that in spite of the difficulty of this passage the challenge should not be watered down. If we love Christ and abide in him we ought not to be sinning *at all*! What a good thing that John has already reminded us back in 2:1–2 that when we do not meet this ideal, God forgives us through the work of Christ.

3:11–24 Love in deed and truth; enjoy assurance

This section begins by recalling 1:1–3 and the love commandment of 2:10. What better way of emphasizing the need for love for our 'brethren' (14) than by drawing the dramatic contrast between Christians and a brother who did not love as he should have done. Cain murdered his brother Abel (Gen. 4:8). The details of that story are not important here. Cain was evil in his actions because he belonged to the evil one. His behaviour showed to all that he did not have eternal life (15), that he was not a child of God.

John then goes on to present us with the example that we should follow: Jesus (16). If we want to know what love really is, then look to Jesus who gave his life for us. Here it becomes clear that the theory about love is simply not enough. The example of Jesus giving himself for us happened in history . . . love must be acted upon and seen. We 'know' love because we have actually experienced the benefits that have come to us through the action of Christ in laying down his life as an atonement for us. While John does not expect us to make atonement for others (only Jesus can do this and he has done it once and for all time), nevertheless, the example of one being able to give himself completely for the sake of another is to be followed. The stark contrast between Jesus and Cain is obvious. It is possible that John was thinking of being prepared to die for each other under persecution, but verse 17 reminds us that the application can be immediate and relevant for any Christian at any time in history.

Verse 18 shows the real nature of this challenge to right living and right love, by suggesting that it is possible for Christians to talk a lot about this subject and yet do very little! (See question 5, p 56.)

Faced with this challenge it is likely that we shall feel condemned (20,21)! We need to be made aware of our sin and we should continue to examine ourselves. However, God's mercy gives us the *assurance* that he has forgiven us and lives in us, and this is the theme to which John now returns. God is greater than our feelings and knows everything about us. His mercy and faithfulness, expounded earlier in the letter, can be relied upon. He will look after his own children. We *do* have an Advocate!

Do you lack this assurance? Then firstly, ask yourself whether you believe in Jesus (23), and whether you desire to love others. If you do, then you 'abide in him' (24a). Notice that you cannot have this love without belief, and this sort of belief will lead naturally into love (see Matt 22:37–39. For further discussion of the relationship between belief and love, see the notes on 5:1–12.) Secondly, do you recognize the presence of the Spirit in your life, not simply in making you aware of your sin, but in helping you to listen to and understand God's word so that you know what he wants for you (4:6)? This also is the evidence that should give you complete assurance. Remember that Paul talks of the Spirit as the 'guarantee' (Eph 1:13–14) of our redemption.

On 3:22, see comments on 5:14.

4:1–21 Reject evil, love God

Several themes raised earlier are now elaborated upon by John. We belong to God, therefore we must distinguish clearly between the teaching of the world, and teaching which is genuinely from God and reveals his desires for his people (1–6). Since we belong to God we must love others who do (7–12). Our assurance lies in the fact that we possess the Spirit and believe in Jesus as the Son of God (13–16). As God is love so we should love God and our brothers (17–21).

If false teachers are to be rejected then we need to be careful to 'test the spirits' (1). Anyone may say they have the Spirit of God. Today many people seek after the miraculous and varied types of spiritual 'experience', so this need to test the spirits is immediately relevant. The existence of false prophets should be of as much concern now as it was to John and to Christ (see Mark 13:6,21–22). Testing for false spirits is done by examining the teaching of all teachers or prophets in some detail. The most important test is whether the 'spirit' *confesses* the true humanity of Jesus and his true divinity (note that 'has come', 2, indicates his pre-existence). Remember that John emphasized this truth of the incarnation at the start of his letter.

The word 'confesses' is important. Even the demons recognized who Jesus was (Mark 5:7), but they did not 'confess' him. They did not believe in him in the sense of giving themselves to him in obedience and faith. Today there are many who preach a message about Jesus and who seem to say the right things. It is the duty of every Christian to test these messages. Do they reflect the *full* message that John has related to us – that Jesus was truly human; that he was truly God; that he will come again as judge; that he was pre-existent and that he is now Lord of all? Christology remains one of the most important ways by which to determine whether someone reflects the Spirit of God or some other spirit. Someone teaching under the guidance of the Holy Spirit will not keep quiet about these truths either but will actively propagate them. Some people, for instance, claim to be inspired by the Spirit and yet never draw attention to Christ, but only to the Spirit. The true work of the Holy Spirit is not to draw attention to himself but to Christ (5:7; John 15:26).

Just as this confession is a test of teachers so it is a test for individual Christians (15–16). Belief in Jesus recognizes that Jesus has been sent by God, who loved us before we loved him (19). The love we are to have for God and for each other arises out of this knowledge. We no longer need have any fear of judgment (18) because we have experienced the love of God. Let us therefore respond in love for God and for each other.

(See question 6, p 56.)

5:1–12 Life in the Son

Sometimes in this letter it has been difficult to see quite what the relationship is between love and faith. Both indicate that we are children of God. In what we have seen so far the order in which they appear in a person's life is best expressed as: **1.** God's love for us; **2.** faith; **3.** our love for God and for each other. This final chapter now helps clarify the issue. Belief in Jesus as the Messiah (Christ) is at the heart of everything. Belief is the dominant idea in the next few verses (1,5, 10 three times, 13), for it is the *condition* of entry, of being born into the family of God (Smalley, p 266; see John 1:12).

John's logic (1) is that belief makes us a child of God, so God is the Father of the believer, and if we love the Father then we should love the other children! In summary it can be said that 'faith and love are inseparable. In God's family, faith in God and love for him and his children are totally integrated' (Kistemaker, p 348).

Again, profession of love for God is not enough (3). Love for God is seen in *keeping his commandments*. We do this not because some law tells us we have to, but simply because *we love God* and want to do his will. Obedience, even arising out of this love, can seem hard work at times, but John encourages us here by reminding us that we do not do these things in our own strength. The faith we have is in Christ (4), and he has overcome the world for us (5). The battle with the sin and disobedience that are so widespread in the world, has already been won by Christ himself when he died on the cross (John 16:33). So we need to make sure that we really do believe in him in practice, not just in theory. The discussion about faith in Jesus as the Son of God (5–13) thus follows logically. But first, note how yet again John has drawn together the necessity for *belief, love* and *obedience*.

There are witnesses to this faith in Christ the Son of God. The 'water' and 'blood' (6) have caused much debate. The most satisfactory explanation is that John is referring here to Jesus' baptism by water and to his death. In verse 8 'the Spirit' heads the list of witnesses which 'are one' ('agree' – RSV), and in 10 we find that these are in fact the witness of God himself 'to his Son'. The witness is to the true human life of Christ and to his true divinity. He 'came' (6) looks to his divine sonship, and the baptism witnesses to his identifying himself with his people and to the Spirit's confirmation that he is God's Son (Mark 1:11). His death witnesses to his true humanity as he died to save his people. Notice that the Spirit 'is' the witness (7). He continues to witness to the truth about Jesus' incarnation through the written word, the preached word and in the hearts and lives of believers.

It is difficult to imagine a more urgent message for the church today. The truth of the incarnation, fundamental to Christianity, is being challenged on all sides. (See question 7, p 56.)

Note: The AV refers to three witnesses on earth and three in heaven. Only a few very late manuscripts have these words.

5:13–21 Christian confidence

These closing verses summarize the letter by pointing out seven things that we 'know' as Christians, and in which we can have confidence.

1. John writes (13) that we may believe in the Son of God (see John 20:31), and know that we have eternal life. Eternal life starts now, when we are born of God, and continues beyond the grave (John 6:40).

2. We know he hears us (14). This picks up on 3:22. As the children of God we can be assured that our Father hears and answers our prayers. But note the condition: 'according to his will'. Even Jesus prayed in this way (Matt 26:39). Our Father answers only as is best for his children, and there is always the possibility, therefore, that he may say 'no'.

3. Knowing this, we also know that 'we have' the requests, that is, God has heard and *does* answer (15).

4. We know a Christian does not sin (18). This also relates back to chapter 3 (see Excursus there), but is closely related to the rest of this section too, for such knowledge as this depends on belief in Jesus, being in the family of God, and thus being in the will of the Father. In Christ our sin is overcome. This is what is meant in 18b: 'He who was born of God' probably refers to Jesus as God's Son who 'keeps' his people from evil (John 10:28; 17:12,15).

5. Verse 19 is a great summary verse of all that John has been saying. It is worth pausing here to reflect again on what he has told us and why it is true. Lack of assurance that we really are 'of God' is serious, for it casts doubt on the protecting and keeping work of Jesus himself.

6. We know the Son of God and, therefore **7.**, we know 'him who is true' (20). John finishes in the way he began this letter; we have fellowship with the Son and with the Father (1:2–3).

Verse 20 comes as a glorious reminder of the gospel which confronts a world that is 'in the power of the evil one' (19). This is the message we must pass on as we too confront the world. We have knowledge of a *person*. Jesus reveals to us the Father, 'the true God'. Being 'in him who is true' reminds us that it is being in Christ that leads to us truly knowing God.

There are two other extremely practical points in this section, not to be overlooked. Firstly, we must not go after any other god or religion (21); that is, we must not look to any source other than Jesus for the knowledge of God. Secondly, if we love our brothers, we should pray for them that they will not sin (16–17). To commit a 'mortal' sin is to set oneself firmly against the gospel, like the antichrists referred to earlier in the letter. John does not linger on this. He is more concerned that we pray for each other as we become caught up in sin. (Look again, in the light of this section, at question 6, p 56.)

2 John: Continue in truth and love

The content of this letter has obvious affinities with the first, in which the themes of love and truth were so prominent. But here a sadness seems to creep into John's message. There is now not just a warning against antichrists but a more definite concern being expressed that this group is threatened and in danger of losing what it has worked for (8).

The trouble is that the deceivers ('antichrist' – 7) have gone out into the world. These were probably the people who left the Johannine churches in 1 John 4:1. But here in 2 John it seems that they have 'gone out' as *missionaries* (see 3 John 7 where the same word is used of Christian missionaries). These people are true antichrists and set out to proclaim their destructive distortion of the gospel.

As we found in 1 John the false teaching centres on the person of Christ. The first concern here is with those who deny the humanity of Jesus (7). But notice the present tense is used here: 'as coming in the flesh' (NIV). This suggests that perhaps the concern was not just with whether Jesus was born a human but whether he *now* has human flesh. Throughout history groups of false teachers have argued that Jesus may have had a divine power between his baptism and death, but the union between human and divine did not last. The New Testament teaches that we have a risen *incarnate* Lord even now. It is because he is incarnate that we can have fellowship with the Son, and so also, through him, with the Father.

There are practical warnings given here that we would do well to heed. For all the talk of 'love' in this letter and in 1 John it is not sentimentality. False teachers are antichrists. Light has nothing to do with darkness. We must not give time or hospitality to such people (10–11). There are no 'ifs' and 'buts' in this command. These people are out to deceive, and we are in *real* danger. Possibly John has in mind an invitation into the church rather than private hospitality, and we should remember that it applies to those who are missionaries against orthodox Christianity not just to those who may have been led astray by others. But let us *never* under-estimate the danger we face when we have contact with such people.

It is worth remembering that there is something inconsistent in praying daily 'Lead us not into temptation', and then proceeding to walk right into it by befriending false teachers.

3 John: A personal letter

Anyone who has had the privilege of leading someone else to Christ will know the joy that is felt at seeing that person continuing in the faith and growing in their knowledge and love of the Lord. There are indications in this, the most personal of John's letters, that he had led Gaius to the Lord (4). In reading this verse it is worth pausing to ask ourselves whether Christians returning from time spent with us would carry back the same message: 'this person follows the truth'. Remember again John's teaching that the truth is not just abstract. Here it is worked out in the life of Gaius (3).

There is an interesting contrast (5–8) with 2 John. There we saw that it is wrong to give hospitality to those who are intent on persuading their hosts of a different 'gospel'. Now an example is held up to us of true and useful hospitality. Gaius has even helped *strangers* on their way. To 'send them on their way' probably involved not only putting people up in the home for a while but also giving them provisions for travelling (Rom 15:24).

At stake here is the whole functioning of the body of Christ (to use Paul's metaphor). Our objective should be to be 'fellow workers in the truth' (8). If *we* are not itinerant missionaries or evangelists, we can still have a role in working with them in the witness of the gospel, even from our homes. (See question 8, p 56.) Note again that the difference between following evil or following good is a motivating factor here (11). We should help fellow Christians so that they do not have to rely on heathen people for help (7). We can hardly maintain our distinctive Christianity if our help comes not from the Lord (through his people) but from the very non-Christians we wish to evangelize.

Diotrephes is a sad example in Gaius' church of the exact opposite. He seems to have been an elder who had refused to take note of an earlier letter John had written. Perhaps the privilege of his position had caused him to become proud, or perhaps he had begun to be influenced by the false teachers. How sad that even in a church watched over by the apostle John, an elder could have gone astray: a salutary reminder of how much we should pray for our elders and leaders.

John ends on a more positive note in commendation of Demetrius (12). Like him, we should 'imitate good'. Christ is our prime example but sometimes we can learn to do good by following others who show the truth to us as Demetrius and Gaius do in this letter (see 1 Cor 11:1).

Questions for further study and discussion on the letters of John

1. What does the word 'fellowship' mean to you, and what is the basis for your fellowship with others?

2. How seriously do you take the fact that it is by your behaviour that others *see* whether or not you are the children of God?

3. What sort of example of love for others does John himself set in his letter?

4. Why is teaching so important? Do you receive enough teaching? If not, what will you do about it?

5. In what ways do you 'love in word or speech' and yet not 'in deed and in truth'?

6. What evidences do you see in your life that give you grounds for assurance and confidence before God?

7. Try to summarize all the truths you have learned that are essential to a proper belief in the incarnate Son of God. In what ways do you find each of these truths being challenged today?

8. How can we offer hospitality to others, as 'co-workers in the truth' (NIV)?

Jude: Introduction

Authorship

It is generally accepted that the author referred to in verse 1 is Jude, the brother of James the Just, that is the half-brother of Jesus (see Mark 6:3). Some people have felt that the letter was written by someone else claiming to be Jude in order to give his letter more authority. If this were the case then it is surprising that a more prominent figure than Jude was not chosen. Also the letter would surely have carried more weight if, instead of referring to himself as the brother of James (1), the pseudonymous writer had mentioned Jesus! In fact the reasons put forward for pseudonymous authorship are far from compelling.

It is possible that Jude wrote with 2 Peter in mind – a point suggested by a number of commentators in the light of the 'reminder' (5) and the 'predictions of the apostles' (17). But for a discussion of the relationship between this letter and 2 Peter, see the introduction to that book.

There is little information in this letter that would indicate at all clearly when it was written. But, assuming it was written by Jude, AD 90 is probably the latest date. Given that the problems faced by Jude concerned the rejection by certain travelling teachers of all moral law, then the date could be as early as the mid-fifties AD when Paul too encountered such problems.

Recipients and opponents

We know virtually nothing about the recipients of this letter. The way in which Jude uses Jewish writings may indicate that the church comprised predominantly Christian converts from Judaism. However, most new Christians from whatever background would be carefully taught from the Old Testament and probably from some of the other Jewish writings, so this is not a conclusive argument.

More easily determined is the particular stance of the false teachers who are the opponents of the truth in this church. Example after example that Jude uses in this brief letter emphasizes the fact that these people despised the law. They were 'antinomian' (Greek: *nomos* = law). This led such people into boasting, causing divisions, and into advocating wrong behaviour in every area of life, especially in sexual ethics.

Purpose and teaching

The purpose of the letter is threefold:

1. Jude seeks to encourage the Christians to whom he is writing. This may have been his sole purpose in writing originally. This purpose is particularly prominent in the opening and the closing verses where there is great stress on the graciousness of God, and his faithfulness in keeping his children from falling (1,24).

2. However, perhaps while he was still thinking about writing to them, he received some disturbing news from the church and so felt it necessary to write appealing to them 'to contend for the faith which was once for all delivered to the saints' (3).

3. Closely tied to the fact that they should contend for the faith is the purpose Jude has of teaching the church from the Scriptures that such problems are not new, and that God has consistently shown he will judge those who teach perversions of the gospel.

It is thus to the graciousness and mercy of God that Jude appeals. The great consolation in the midst of attack from heretics is that God looks after his own and will indeed keep them.

There is both warning and consolation to be found in the fact that God judges evildoers. We should be warned that perverting God's truth leads to judgment and that people who do this exist *inside* the church. We must neither pervert God's grace nor must we be misled by such false teachers for decisive and final judgment will come. The consolation in this is that evil will not go on for ever, and with judgment comes the presentation of Christians 'before the presence of [God's] glory with rejoicing' (24).

Outline

1–2   Greeting
3–4   The reason for the letter
5–19   Examples of sin and judgment on antinomian groups in the past
20–23 Jude appeals to the Christians
24–25 Doxology

Jude: Contents

1–4 The grace of God

While most of this letter addresses the perversion (4) of God's grace, Jude's opening verses stress the fulness of his grace in two lists of three ideas (1–2).

Verse 1

1. As *'called'* people they know that God is in control of everything in this life and that *he* cares for them. The called are the ones who enter God's covenant community. These are the ones to whom God's promises are made, and the ones for whom Christ died.

2. Such people are clearly *'beloved* in God the Father'. This extremely close relationship they have with the Father should bring them confidence in him.

3. Being *'kept'* for Jesus Christ calls to mind John 17 where Jesus prayed to the Father that he would 'keep' his followers: the chosen. It introduces us to the final goal towards which God is working in our lives: life in heaven with the Father and the Son.

Bauckham has pointed to a possible Old Testament background to these ideas in Isaiah, for instance: 'called' (Isa 41:9), 'loved' (Isa 43:4), 'kept' (Isa 42:6).

Verse 2

Mercy, peace and love, united here in a Christian greeting, also look back to the covenant promises of God to his people. Mercy is virtually synonymous with grace. Peace looks to the *shalom*, or blessing of permanent peace, promised to the covenant children.

In asking that these blessings of God be 'multiplied' to them Jude shows that covenantal mercy is not static. The church needs God's continuing upholding mercy and love.

False teachers have literally infiltrated the church. 'Long ago . . . designated for this condemnation' is not easy to understand. But perhaps in the light of the Old Testament examples Jude is going to give us, he is saying that Jewish prophecy from long ago can be applied to this situation in the church. In that the Old Testament reveals God's purpose and plans it is quite true to say that God long ago marked out these people for the sort of condemnation that others have also received.

'Faith' (3) refers to the system of truth in which they believed (ie the gospel message). 'Once for all delivered' is an important truth that needs to be grasped again at the end of the twentieth century. False teaching is tested and checked against the apostolic faith delivered *once* by the apostles. Their foundational truth can never be changed by anyone (see Gal 1:6–9; 2 John 9).

What we need today is not some new message. All that is needed is the gospel and the apostolic interpretation of the facts. So often sects claim to have 'extra' truth. We can know they are wrong because the great truth is that we are saved in just the same way as those Christians to whom Jude was writing.

4–16 Perverting the grace of God

The infiltrators were propounding two false doctrines that were closely related (4b).

The first mentioned is 'licentiousness'. It seems that the teaching 'saved by grace alone' was being perverted into something like: 'Let us do what we like, we are saved anyway'. Or maybe they believed that their souls were saved and so they could do what they liked with their bodies. Either way, God's moral law was abused.

The second doctrine concerned Christology. In practical terms their perversion of the grace of God was a denial of Christ as Master. To be involved in sexual immorality is to deny that Christ is your Master – the one who has placed rightful demands upon his subjects. In other words, Jesus' authority is being denied by these actions.

Perhaps this sort of teaching began quite simply, as so often today, with teachers who were unwilling to be dogmatic in their stand for biblical attitudes against the pressures of a syncretistic society. Such leaders give their people exactly what their 'itching ears' want to hear (2 Tim 4:3).

Jude now presents a series of examples from the past of incidents that reflect similar problems, and the consequent judgment of God on the sinful. Verses 5–7 give examples which are then applied in the present tense in verses 8 and 10.

The wilderness events are the most common examples in Jewish literature of what happens when people do not obey the Lord. The Israelites were saved from Egypt but then sinned (eg Num 14:1–38; 26:64–65). Reference to the angels (6) is probably a reference to Genesis 6:1–4. 1 Enoch 6–19 (see Excursus) maintains that the sin of the 'sons of God', who it says were angels, was sexual perversion. The third example, of Sodom and Gomorrah, also emphasizes sexual sin. (The words 'strange flesh' in Greek are translated 'unnatural lust'.) These sad examples of sin all point to the fact that God judges such things with eternal fire (7).

The other examples continue to show God's law being rejected in various ways. The 'love feasts' might refer to the communion. Even these times of fellowship were being distorted by this perverted teaching. The descriptions of those who pervert God's grace leave nothing to the imagination (10,12,13,16)! The book of Enoch is quoted to show that God will convict the sinners (see Excursus).

This dire warning of the dangers of sexual sin spans the centuries. It is doubtful whether any other age has seen the promiscuous freedom we see today. Do we realize how important it is to speak firmly and decisively to these issues?

Excursus: The use of 1 Enoch

It is obvious from reading Jude's letter that he relies to some extent on intertestamental literature and ideas. The background for these ideas can be found within the Old Testament, but the detail Jude uses and the way in which he builds his arguments depends especially on a good knowledge of 1 Enoch. 1 Enoch is not in our canon of the Old Testament and is a clearly pseudonymous work (not really written by Enoch). Thus a question asked by many is this: Did Jude regard 1 Enoch as fully inspired by God and prophetic, in the way that it was most surely regarded in some Jewish circles around the time he was writing? A number of points are worth noting:

1. There is no particular reason why Jude in citing one text is thereby giving full and binding authority to the *whole* book of 1 Enoch. Scholars have noted that Paul can quote from entirely secular sources; for example he quotes from Cleanthes and Aratus in Acts 17:28, and he quotes Menander in 1 Corinthians 15:33 and Epimenides in Titus 1:12. He does not thereby give canonical or final authority to their words.

2. Perhaps we should say that those quoted words, in that they are affirmed by a canonical writer, are the word of God because the Spirit has inspired *that* writer to say them. That is, these quotations can be accepted as part of the word of God given to us, not because the work from which they come is either canonical or written by Enoch, but because, under the Spirit's instruction, Jude himself took the words and applied them correctly.

3. It is certainly possible that Jude understood what was written in the book of Enoch to be, at least in places, 'prophecy'. It is also likely that he believed the book to be an accurate interpretation of the Old Testament canon and therefore worth quoting.

A paraphrase of Jude's intention here might go something like this: 'Here is a book you know well; it contains much that is useful and it is to be respected. We can learn a number of things from it. In some places we can learn from its interpretation of parts of the Old Testament; in other places the men of God who wrote this book spoke prophetically from the Lord.'

In citing it, Jude thereby gives the book itself no more authority than we might give, say, to Spurgeon, when we recognize that on a particular verse, and under the Spirit's guidance, he has opened up the canonical word to us.

17–25 To the only God

There are two signs (19) that these teachers do not possess the Holy Spirit in spite of their claims to have visions and dreams (8): they create divisions and they behave like animals (10, ie with no moral inhibitions). Today, teachers of new and easy forms of Christianity are claiming similarly to be messengers of the Spirit. Here we are given two fairly straightforward tests by which we can judge them. Do they divide believers – perhaps suggesting one group is spiritually superior to others? Or, as has happened in some well-publicized cases recently, do they lead people into moral sin?. Sadly, one certainly does not have to look far for leaders who cause divisions.

So Jude now shows how to apply the faith, delivered 'once and for all', to the situation in the church. The apostles, he says, had predicted that this would happen. The concept of the 'last time' is similar to the 'last days' (see on 2 Peter 3:1–9). This is the age of the Messiah, the age in which the prophecies of old can and must be applied to the church. We must do so with the same vigour and earnestness today as Jude did so long ago.

So Jude now wants these people to begin to look at ways of dealing with the situation and what they are to do is to apply the apostolic and prophetic word.

How are they to do this? Jude looks back to the 'faith' (3). He tells them to build themselves up on that faith. This does not simply mean struggling to 'feel' closer to God. What Jude is saying is that the apostolic faith will sustain anyone: it is unchangeable. The faith is not just what I believe, or what I am prepared to put into action at this moment; it is established and can never be changed. Here is something objective that they can continue to study and learn thoroughly so that they will be able to see heresy in the future as soon as it rears its most ugly head. They should study the sayings of the apostles and they should apply them, and only them, to their day and age. Praying towards this end will indeed be 'praying in the Spirit' (20 – not a reference to ecstatic speech). What a warning this is for us: a warning and yet an encouragement! If they had known God's word better they would have stood a better chance of 'contending' for it. But they did not know it well, and Satan soon took advantage of this situation.

'Keep yourselves' reminds the readers of their responsibility, not to earn their salvation, but to make sure that they obey God (see John 15:9–10). Part of that responsibility is also to evangelize (22–23) wherever possible.

The wonderful doxology (24–25) that ends this letter is another of those treasures of Scripture. It tells us why we should contend for the faith, and into whose power we should commit ourselves if we wish to be successful at the task: 'to the only God, our Saviour . . .'

Questions for further study and discussion on the letter of Jude

1. Why is it important to believe in the 'once for all delivered' faith?

2. Do you think the grace of God is being perverted among Christians you know? If so, how?

3. Sexual sin and perversion is especially highlighted in this letter.

a) Does your church do enough teaching on this subject?

b) If you have children, how do you see your parental responsibility in this area? For example, would you rather they did not read passages of Scripture like this or like Romans 1:26–27 so that they will not ask awkward questions?

c) Remember that for those who have fallen in sin in this area of their lives, verses 24 and 25 offer great comfort. What is the remedy for serious sin like this?

Revelation: Introduction

Undoubtedly it is strange that the one book in the Bible that claims to be an 'apocalypse' ('unveiling' or 'revelation') remains, for us in the twentieth century, probably the most obscure of all the books in the Bible. Many Christians have hardly bothered to examine the work beyond the first three chapters, and others who have spent much study in its intricacies have occasionally ended up splitting churches over issues to do with the 'last things'!

The commentary which you are about to study cannot hope to do justice to this intriguing book, but hopefully it will stimulate thinking and serve as an encouragement to go on learning from a wonderful and important part of God's word.

Authorship and dating

The Apocalypse (Revelation) was a revelation given to one called John (1:1), by God, through an angel. Traditionally from earliest times it has been assumed that this was the apostle John. In fact it is not possible to be certain of this from the text. John does not say that he was 'the apostle'. Some scholars have argued that the Greek used is very poor compared with other Johannine writings. Having said that, the use the author makes of the Old Testament and even the Targums (Aramaic versions of the Old Testament) suggests strongly that the author was a Palestinian Jew who knew well what went on in the synagogue. Such a description would fit the apostle well. Elsewhere he says that what he writes is a 'prophecy' (1:3; 22:6–7,18–19) and throughout assumes a level of authority that was typical of the apostles. Also, much of the way the author discusses theology is reminiscent of the way ideas are presented in the Gospel of John and the epistles.

To some extent the dating of the book affects the authorship question. If it was written after the mid-nineties AD, then it is most unlikely that the apostle John was still alive. Some have suggested that it was written shortly after Nero's time of persecution. Nero reigned from AD 54 to AD 68. In AD 64 Rome was burned and Nero, who was probably responsible for the fire himself, blamed the Christians for it. Many, including Peter and Paul, were killed and tortured in ways which horrified even the Romans. References to persecution in this book could fit such horror (see chs 11, 13, 17:6). The reference to 'Babylon' (Rome) being burned (17:16) would further support this dating. It is also said that the idea of the 'beast' returning (13:3,12; 17:8,11–12) indicates a period shortly after Nero's suicide when the fable spread that Nero would return. Further support for a date prior to AD 70, proposed by some, is that 11:1–3 indicates the temple is still standing but Jerusalem is in the hands of evil people. (The temple was destroyed in AD 70.)

However, most people believe the book was written during Domitian's rule (AD 81–96). Although there is little evidence of wide-scale persecution at this time, Domitian did assume to himself the title 'Lord and God', which might explain some of John's deep concerns. The early theologian, Irenaeus, talked of John seeing his vision 'not a long time ago . . . at the end of Domitian's reign'.

There is no need to assume a date *later* than the early to mid-nineties, in which case John the apostle could still have been the author in his old age.

Prophecy and apocalypse

Even a cursory glance at the book from chapter 4 onwards reveals a different style or type of literature from much else to be found in the Bible. This means that we must be careful how we read the letter, and that we try to do justice to a form of literature which seems alien to us in the twentieth century.

Firstly, it should be noted how very indebted John is to the Old Testament, especially in those sections where symbolism is important. In fact, much of the symbolism of Revelation is an extension of that already found in the Old Testament prophets like Daniel and Ezekiel. We should also keep in mind that this book was written as a letter to a particular group of churches. As a prophet John is determined to proclaim God's word, specifically to those people. He brings them encouragement at a time of difficulty, for Christians were either suffering at that time, or needed to be warned that what had happened before (under Nero) was likely to happen again. John assures his people of God's sovereign rule (kingdom) right now in the *present*, while bringing consolation with promises of the parousia (second coming). In this sense we are dealing with a prophecy similar to those found in the Old Testament: proclamations of God's present and future workings with his people, comfort to those who are oppressed, and warnings to those turning back from the truth to the evil of the world. John, working under the Spirit's inspiration like the prophets, brings a message that is always relevant. It is no doubt for all these reasons that John sees himself as writing prophecy.

Secondly, this work is an 'apocalypse' ('revelation', 1:1), which is a word primarily applied to a type of Jewish writing which often had its roots in Old Testament prophecy, but which concentrated on two or three major themes. These would be, for instance, 'the Day of the Lord', and the complete sovereignty of God even in the most severe times of distress for his people. History was seen as leading to a climax when God would come and separate good from evil, 'this age' from the next, light from darkness. Normally these writings were written in the name of the heroes of ancient Israelite history, eg the books of Enoch, or the Assumption of Moses. Another of the characteristics of this literature was that it was pessimistic and even deterministic about this world. The only hope was the future in another world.

Revelation shares some apocalyptic elements with these other Jewish works especially, of course, in its great use of symbolism and of visions. John, for instance, also sees history in two ages and looks for the coming day of judgment and a new life in a new heaven and earth where evil will be banished.

There are also substantial differences between John's Revelation and apocalyptic literature. Ralph Martin lists four points (*New Testament Foundations* [Vol 2], Exeter: Paternoster, 1978; pp 372–373):

1. This work is not attributed to some great person of the past but to a living person called 'John'.

2. Revelation is a letter, not just a literary masterpiece. Chapters 2–3 and 22:6–21 suggest it was to be read in specific local churches.

3. The consolation offered by John is not remote and futuristic but is presented in terms of the *present* reality of God's kingdom and an assurance of the second coming of *Christ*.

4. While John does see heavenly realities (eg 4:1), these are not simply 'other-worldly' but are related closely to earthly events and the present situation of the church.

John is primarily, therefore, a pastor in a real situation about which he is not pessimistic. For him the victory is *already* to be found in the Lamb who was slain (ch 5). This victory is being worked out by the church in *this* world. There is even victory to be found in martyrdom, as such a witness to the truth of Christ (who *has* authority and *has* come) demonstrates God's victory (12:11).

The book is therefore to be seen as a pastoral letter full of the characteristics of Old Testament prophecy, and incorporating some of the style of apocalyptic literature – but not necessarily its theology.

Interpretation

Recognizing the prophetic and apocalytpic traits of this letter is an important starting point as we seek to understand the relevance of John's message for us today. Even so, we must recognize that there have been different 'schools' of thought on how best to interpret Revelation.

1. Some say that the book simply describes in vivid symbolism *the ongoing struggle between good and evil* in which, eventually, Christianity triumphs. The tendency here is that everything is 'spiritualized'. There is no real prophecy or prediction of future events but simply a description of the continuing battle. There is, of course, considerable truth in this position, for part of the appeal and relevance of the book lies in the fact that each successive generation of Christians can identify with so much that it relates.

However, it underestimates the immediate relevance to those to whom John was writing and eliminates the possibility of the direct identification of some of the symbols with events either in the future or in the history of the church.

2. A second school of thought interprets Revelation exclusively in terms of *a tract for John's own age*. This view stresses the contemporary nature of the events described. All the events referred to and disclosed in symbolic language would have been clearly understood by the recipients as pertaining to their situation. Some then go on to say that the prophecies relating to Christ's second coming and the destruction of the Roman Empire turned out to be mistaken. The usefulness of this position is that it draws attention to the fact that John did write for a specific audience at a specific time. Many of his symbols probably were understood by his readers in a way in which we cannot understand them. Time and again John clearly seems to have in mind the Roman Empire and Rome itself. However, the book claims more than contemporary significance and this view does not do justice to the predictive element of the work.

3. Another way in which the book has been interpreted, and which was largely followed by the Reformers like Luther and Calvin, is to regard it as *a symbolic description of the history of the church*. Once the symbols are deciphered then church history can be understood. 'Babylon' is seen as Rome, but not just the Rome of John's day. For Luther it became papal Rome as well. This position certainly takes prophecy seriously and tries to fit John's symbols and prophecies into the history of the church, or vice versa. The real problem faced by such a view is the lack of consensus as to what is actually being described in different sections of the book. As Gundry says (p 346), those taking this position 'have variously identified the locusts from the abyss in 9:1ff with the Vandals, Goths, Persians, Mohammedans, heretics and others'.

4. Fourthly, there is a view of the book that is sometimes called 'futurist'. From chapter 4 onwards Revelation deals with *what will happen in the future*, just before and at the time of Christ's second coming. The symbolism and descriptions largely concern themselves with a future time of troubles and sufferings for Christians called 'the tribulation', after which Christ will return and judge the world, and eternal life with Christ will begin for the righteous.

People who adopt this position are usually *pre-millennialists* (see below). Some in this camp believe that Christians will, in fact, be taken away from the earth before this period of tribulation begins, that is, before the events related from chapter 6 onwards ('pre-tribulationism').

If this particular form of pre-millennialism should seem to make much of the book irrelevant, some draw together their futurist views with that given in 1) above, that each generation continues to see the ongoing struggle between Christ and his followers and Satan.

Among evangelicals in the USA probably the majority adopt some form of futurist position. It is also widely held in other English-speaking countries. There are many other Christians, however, equally devoted to Scripture, who hold to one or other of the remaining three views given above. This alone is perhaps an indication that while we should search the Scriptures under the Spirit's guidance and come to understand as much as possible, it may be wise to refrain from being over-dogmatic in our views on this subject!

More must be said about different approaches to this book, however, for nowadays certain terms are used that are often misunderstood. While this commentary only makes occasional reference to these rather technical words it is important to know what they mean, especially if this book is to provide a basis for group discussion.

Pre-millennialism

This view was mentioned above. The basic proposition (although there are variations on this) is that Revelation and other passages of Scripture point to the establishing of the Davidic kingdom of Israel by Christ when he returns. He is to come as 'the Davidic King' to rule in a time of righteousness and peace over all the world, thus fulfilling prophecies in the Old Testament that are regarded as not yet fulfilled. This reign will be for 1000 years (*millennium* – sometimes taken literally and sometimes understood symbolically of an extended period of time), after which will come a rebellion, led by Satan, which Christ will defeat. The final judgment will then take place followed by eternal life with Christ for the righteous.

Post-millennialism

This view is not often found today but was held by some of the Puritans and became important in the great missionary movements of the last century. Some Reformed groups hold a variation of it today. Here the millennium (1000-year rule) is understood symbolically. Christ will return *after* (post-) a great, final age in history when Christ will reign spiritually in and through his church. During this time much of the world will be converted.

Amillennialism

Some say this view is the most commonly held position outside the USA. Christ's 1000-year rule is taken symbolically to represent the *present* rule of Christ, that between the resurrection/ascension and the second coming. Seated now at the right hand of God, Christ rules over the earth and especially in the hearts of Christians in his church. At a time which the Father will choose, he will return to bring judgment, and then the righteous will begin their resurrected life with Christ.

The reader should try to come to the book of Revelation with an open mind. Of course, this is never completely possible but he should, as always, seek the Spirit's help in understanding what God was saying through John to his own day and age and to ours. At times this commentary draws attention to the considerable differences of opinion among biblical commentators. However, it is committed to the belief that, while talking of many things yet to happen, the Spirit *intends this work to be directly relevant to us.*

Theology

John's indebtedness to the Old Testament was mentioned above, but, first and foremost, he is indebted to the gospel of Christ. The links with Jesus' own teaching are numerous. The person of Jesus as Lamb, ruler, creator, Son of God, Word of God and, above all, King, is at the heart of this message.

As is so clearly seen in the Gospel of John, Jesus carries out the will of the Father but is also equal with him. In reading Revelation the equality of the Father and Son is clear (see 11:15 where the kingdom belongs to the Father and the Son, or compare 4:11 and 5:12). Jesus is worshipped and praised. The consolation for suffering people lies in the assurance that the Lamb was slain and that the Root (son) of David (5:5) will come again and will conquer evil.

People have objected to the harsh, cold descriptions of the wrath of God that are found here, but such perceptions are wide of the mark. John's concern is to show that there is consolation in the fact that one day evil will be totally defeated. This fact gives hope for today, but more than that it gives assurance that God is at all times in control. The devil (Satan, the serpent, the dragon) will never be able to destroy the worship of God, even in this day and age.

On the negative side this concern of John with evil and God's wrath serves as a perpetual reminder to us of the reality of evil and of its power in this world, and the seriousness with which it should be regarded by the church. Only the second coming of Christ will relieve God's people of the need for vigilance in this area. However, as will be seen later, it would be wrong to suggest that this book is all about sin and wrath. As J Sweet puts it so clearly (p 51), 'the structure of the book does make the severity of chapters 6–20 subordinate to the pictures of Creation and Redemption in 4 and 5, and of healing and fulfilment in 21:1–22:5'.

There is a belief throughout this work that Christ is to come suddenly and even soon. This is a conviction found in many places in the New Testament. John was not 'mistaken' simply because the parousia did not happen in his lifetime; rather we, too, should adopt the same stance. Each day must be lived as one day closer to the great day for which we long. John's is the view of a prophet. The time of that day is not stated, but John has seen it in his vision. Christ and all the apostles have talked of it, and it is at the heart of the Christian gospel.

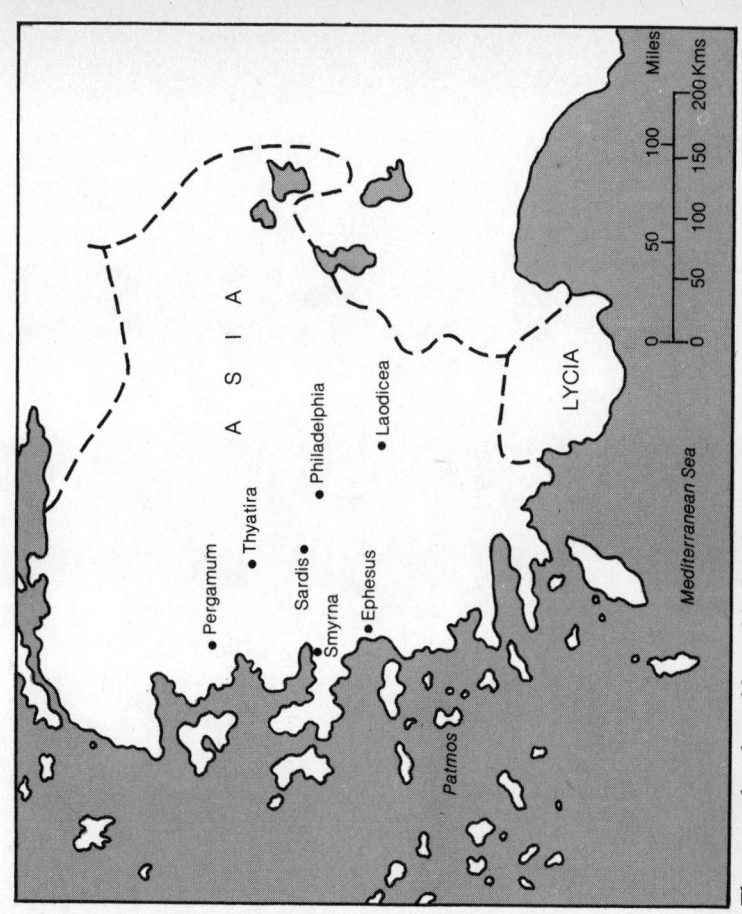

The seven churches addressed in Revelation

79

Revelation: Contents

1:1–20 A revelation for seven churches

John's revelation, received on the island of Patmos possibly during a period of exile for being a Christian leader, concerned Jesus Christ and the future. He calls this a 'prophecy' (3 – see Introduction), which not only refers to prediction but also to teaching and exhortation that comes from God.

The revelation from God came through an angel, and in the form of visions, while John was 'in the Spirit' (10; 4:2; 17:3; 21:10). This may indicate a trance-like state or simply a time when the Spirit spoke to him through these visions or dreams. This word of God was to be delivered to the seven churches (11), and it should be borne in mind that this refers to the whole book, not just chapters 2 and 3.

The descriptions of both God the Father and the Son are particularly outstanding in this chapter. The Father's eternity is stressed (4). The 'seven spirits' may describe the perfection of the Holy Spirit, but certainly look to God's active work (3:1). In v 8 he is described as 'the Alpha and the Omega' and as 'the Almighty' – a title repeated a number of times in this letter, especially drawing attention to his divine sovereignty from all eternity into the eternal future. The fact that God is sovereign is of great importance in this work for in this fact lies the final great hope of Christians. Evil has been defeated by God, in spite of appearances.

The descriptions of Jesus are also of great significance, for God's purposes for his people are worked out through his Son. Again the particular aspects of his work that are mentioned are all designed to bring encouragement to the recipients. They are in his hands, and under his dominion and protection, and he is to come in glory (5–7).

In verses 12–20 we begin immediately to get a taste of the vivid imagery and symbolism that pervades most of the book. Here in verse 20 John gives us help in understanding the seven stars and lampstands mentioned in verses 12–16. But the main point of these verses is to set the context in which the prophecy is given. Christ the Lord is here described as 'the son of man', a figure drawn from Daniel 7:13. He is the one coming in great triumph (7), and yet he is *among* the churches (13). He has attributes usually ascribed to God (compare 8 and 17b). Here is the one with whom the final victory lies and who sustains the churches even in the present. It is precisely because Jesus is the son of man to whom belongs the dominion and power that neither John (17) nor his readers should fear for what is to happen.

Our context today remains the same. We may not all be suffering the same persecution as these seven churches were, but we live with a certainty that Jesus has been given the rule over all, and he is with us now.

2:1–7 Ephesus

The popularity of these letters among preachers is not surprising given their obvious practical relevance to the modern church. At the start of each letter Christ, as the sender, is referred to in terms used in chapter 1. Noting that the same injunction (that the 'churches' should hear the Spirit) ends each letter, it is clear that all the churches were to learn from each other's situation.

One of the most famous ideas to emerge from them is found in this first letter: 'you have abandoned the love you had at first' (4 – see Jer 2:2 where Israel faces a parallel situation). It is probably the experience of all Christians that after conversion they are initially 'in love' with the Lord in a way which seems to fall off later on. The image of 'lovers' is just the one Christ wants us to have. But here a church is the subject not an individual.

The Ephesian church was bearing up well under the onslaught of false 'apostles', as they 'endured' or persevered – an important recurring theme in this letter. Christians should persevere to the end, as tribulation and living in the kingdom go hand in hand in this age (1:9). This they were doing by standing fast in their faith, rightly testing for false teaching, and working really hard to do what they had been taught (2). But their first love was missing! Three things must be done to restore that love (5):

1. They are to 'remember' what things used to be like. Recalling the 'honeymoon' will no doubt motivate them to seek afresh that love.

2. They are to 'repent': to change their whole life before the Lord and turn it around to face the other way.

3. Finally, they are to 'do the works' they did at first. This does not mean that they are to earn their way back into favour and love. True repentance involves showing the fruit of repentance. Their life will need to be changed in fact, not just in theory.

The threat is that the church in that area will cease to be. Jesus 'is coming' (not 'will come'). It is not clear whether John has in mind Christ's judgment of the church at his second coming, or whether continuing present judgment is envisaged.

Many local churches get to this point. Dead orthodoxy, works without love, separation from others for its own sake rather than for love for the Lord; all this is common. In the end the church is no better than a moralistic, educated club. Repentance is required of the whole church. Is Jesus' prophecy of Matthew 24:11–12 coming true in *our* local churches as well?

The rewards mentioned at the end of each letter prefigure the themes of chs 21 and 22 which centre on the new heavens and the new earth. What a prospect!

2:8–17 Smyrna and Pergamum

In these following messages to the churches the Lord makes it clear that he knows the situation of each intimately, a point which should be reassuring and challenging for us in our churches today. The son of man is in the midst of the lampstands (1:13). Recent scholarship has shown just how intimately known they were.

For example, it may have been particularly suitable for the church at Smyrna to hear the words of Christ 'who died and came to life' (8), as that was the way the town itself seems to have been described after an earlier destruction and then rebuilding. The town was very wealthy and this clearly contrasted with the poverty of the Christian community. Non-biblical sources point to the existence of a sizeable and well-established Jewish community. The town was famous for its games, and thus a reward of the 'crown of life' was especially appropriate to a group of Christians who seemed to be missing out on all the world had to offer. It was also a particularly expansive honour given in Smyrna to special citizens. Christians who, because of their faithfulness to the Lord, would never receive such a temporal crown, and who faced the possibility of death, would have been most encouraged with this prospect of a crown of life. The reward is quite definite: these people though tested, will come through this limited period of severe tribulation ('ten days' expresses the limitation) and *shall not* go to eternal damnation. God will uphold them.

Thus Jesus expresses concern in a way which shows not just general concern for people, but special and personal concern. He cares for our churches and knows our situation and trials, sins and successes.

Pergamum was an important city and a great cultural centre, but it was also very pagan, the first city to encourage worship of the emperor. It was fittingly called the place 'where Satan's throne is'. In the face of death the church maintained the faith. As some died by the sword it would be reassuring to know that Jesus had the sharp two-edged sword. Final judgment that matters (16) and real security lie with him alone.

Here we learn something of the Nicolaitan heresy (also at verse 6). For Balaam's sin compare Numbers 31:15–17 with 25:1–3. The main problem here was a temptation to pagan worship and joining in the sacrificial meals which were times of idol worship and probably sexual licence (see Num 25:2b). The problem of accommodating to the pressures of the world around is well known to us today as well. We 'fit in' with the world's demands and pressures in our churches in ways which are evil – and which we may not even recognize as serious.

Again, repentance is required. The battle to remain faithfully living out the gospel is real, but the victor will receive God's gifts of blessing (symbolized in the manna). Many have speculated on the stone and the name. It seems that the name will be a secret between God and the victor that describes the victor's character – a special and very personal reward (see Isa 62:2).

2:18–3:6 Thyatira and Sardis

Thyatira was the least significant town. Some there remained faithful, and the church contrasts with Ephesus in that its current works are better than the first!

Jesus' name, 'Son of God', comes from Psalm 2:7 and looks forward to the reward (27) where that Psalm is quoted. It was appropriate to a town where coins circulated showing the deification of Domitian's son, 'seated on a globe surrounded by seven stars' (Hemer, p 116). Reference to 'bronze feet' recalls the town's particular trade in metallic work. Again and again Jesus gives evidence of this careful, close knowledge of the towns, showing that he is in complete control, and in their midst. He supersedes anything the world has to offer. In the face of the world's power, real power belongs to Jesus (26–27).

From the story of Jezebel (1 Kings 16:31–33; 2 Kings 9:22) the issue again seems to have concerned compromise with the world in terms of idol worship. It has been suggested that business-people like Lydia (Acts 16:14–15) would have had to join trade guilds, membership of which involved eating in the temples of idols. Whatever the situation, a false prophetess was persuading people into immorality. The time for repentance seems to be past in this case, but there is still time for some of those who are being led astray by her ideas – 'who commit adultery with her' (22). Her 'children' were those totally committed to her ways. Those who were trying to remain faithful were encouraged by the reminder that the saints would share in the rule of the Messiah (26,27). The morning star (Venus) symbolizes messianic victory (see 22:16).

Jesus has to call the church at Sardis back to the apostolic faith (3). There is no clear indication of direct opposition to the gospel, but the Christians had moved away from the truth, particularly in their *practice* of Christianity. Their situation paralleled the history of the town, which had twice been conquered through surprise night attack. There is encouragement for those faithful people who still remain (4); their reward is that they will walk with Jesus in victory robes of white. That Jesus 'confesses' people means that he will uphold them on the judgment day (Rev 20:11–15; Matt 10:32).

Others believed this church was 'alive', but it was dead. How many modern churches are in that category? Note the commands: 'Awake', 'strengthen what remains', 'remember then what you received', 'keep that', 'repent'.

Very many people today will recognize their own church in one of these letters. Sometimes our own part in putting things right can seem so insignificant and hopeless, but there are two things to remember:

1. Most of these letters give clear instructions as to how to repent and what to do to get back on the right track.

2. With Christ's help we can and will 'conquer', and rewards await us. Synthesis and compromise with the world are *not* Christian options.

3:7–13 Philadelphia

Smyrna and Philadelphia were the only churches to receive no condemnation or discipline. Calling Jesus the 'true one' and reference to his having the 'key of David', stands in direct contrast to what the Jews would have said of him (9). Isaiah 22:19–22 undoubtedly gives rise to the idea of the 'key of David' and the 'door'. Perhaps Jesus also has in mind the same old debate with the Jews that he had during his lifetime: Who holds the keys to the kingdom (1:18; Matt 23:13)? Who are the real people of God? The Jews closed the synagogue in the faces of the Christians, but in fact it is Christ himself who holds the door open to the kingdom, and these weak and powerless people have direct access to the kingdom of the Messiah, son of David (7–8).

Notice how strong Jesus is in his attack, calling the Jews 'of Satan' and liars (9; John 8:44). Trying to stop people entering the kingdom of God is the whole purpose of Satan. Those Jews were thus furthering the work of Satan in the same way that pagans do (Rom 3:9–10). The Jews had been warned in the Old Testament that if they persisted in sin the Gentiles would receive all the covenant promises (see Rev 21:23–26). This point is also made by Paul in Romans where he musters text after text to show that when Jews did not believe, Gentiles would inherit the promises (Rom 9:25–33; 10:19–21; 15:9–12).

Very sadly there will come a time when these people of Satan will recognize, too late, that it is Christians, and not them, whom Jesus has loved (9; Phil 2:10–11). There will be many other groups who will join the unbelieving Jews in that day. It is worth remembering, at a time in the church when the uniqueness of Christ and his claims upon us are despised, that Jesus himself does not avoid announcing the bad news of judgment.

The good news here is that he will keep the people of this church from the 'hour of trial' (10). 'Trial' in the Bible can be used of testing and refining the elect (2:10), or it can look towards the judgment of God on unbelief. Here it is judgment and the wrath of God that seem to be in mind, though there is great debate about the particular time of trial. There is no special reason to assume that these Christians will be *removed* from the situation before the trial occurs (some suggest that the 'rapture' is in mind). They may well be protected *in* it and *through* it (John 17:15). 'Those who dwell upon the earth' refers in this book to evil people (6:10; 8:13 etc). They are to be the subject of this particular 'trial'.

The joy and comfort of this letter is that even in trials brought about by God for the purposes of judgment, still Christians are kept by Christ. How much more will he keep us and care for us in the minor trials that we experience day by day even now!

3:14–22 Laodicea

It is worth simply listing some of the points of contact Jesus makes with the local situation in Laodicea, though space prohibits much comment.

1. *Cold and hot* refer to the local water supply. Laodicea was renowned for water that tasted bad and which could make one sick (15–16). The hot medicinal waters of Hierapolis, visible across the valley, or the cold refreshing waters of Colossae up the road were preferable. ('Hot' and 'cold' are thus both *positive* attributes.)

2. *I am rich* looks to the pride and wealth of the Laodiceans. In AD 60 they had suffered a great earthquake but had refused to accept financial help from Rome for reconstruction work: 'I need nothing' (17) was their attitude. Jesus says they are 'poor' and he offers them the best refined gold.

3. His description of their *blindness* contrasts with the fact that Laodicea was a well-known medical centre, that appears to have been famous for its eye ointment. Jesus offers them eye-salve (18).

4. Their *nakedness* contrasts with this prosperous town's reputation for providing good clothing. They were especially known for black wool clothing from sheep reared in that area: a contrast with the *white* raiment Jesus supplies.

5. Local superstition possibly believed that the wearing of *white garments* would lead to death, as corpses were buried in white. What a difference from the white robe of righteousness given by Jesus to those who *live* in the kingdom (4:4)!

6. Laodicea was a city where the Romans had billeted their soldiers and requisitioned hospitality from the locals: a contrast with the way *Christ gently approaches them* (20). Perhaps even the reference to the knocking on the door would have brought to the Laodicean mind the picture of the city gate, closed against enemies and undesirables each night.

No other church receives such condemnation as this. It is clear that Jesus knows his churches intimately. He knows that we, too, so easily become complacent and over-confident in the light of our past successes. Does our church rely on its money, its great leaders or its building programme for its status? Let us remember that all the committees, and all our twentieth-century church structures, will achieve nothing if we are not entirely relying on Jesus, recognizing him to be in our midst, and looking to him for his will for us. Have we as Christians (note that verse 20 is still addressed to the church and *Christians* in the church) closed the door on the very one who is our Lord?

Let us thank God that he is gracious enough to discipline us too (19), in order to bring us to repentance.

4:1–11 The holy Creator

This chapter is to be read with a sense of awe and wonder. The first section of the book finished with a vision of Jesus seated on the throne with his Father. Judgment and mercy have been combined in the letters to the churches, but now the scene shifts from the present world of Near Eastern cities to heaven itself and the future that *must* be (1).

It is not possible to interpret accurately all these pictures of what happens in heaven, but some things do become quite clear as the chapter unfolds. It is rightly suggested by some that chapters 4 and 5 are the foundation for all that is to follow in this book. In chapter 4 God is described as holy and worthy to be praised because he is the creator (11); and in chapter 5 the focus is on the Lamb who is worthy to be praised as God who redeems. This sovereign lordship of God in creation and redemption is going to be crucial to understanding the rest of the visions of judgment and destruction. God is indeed judge but he is also utterly faithful to his promises and does redeem his people.

The throne is the centre of this vision, symbolizing God's sovereignty and his judicial role. The descriptions that follow recall some of the other great visions in Scripture (see, for instance, Ezek 1; Isa 6; Dan 7). The idea of a rainbow surrounding the throne (see Ezek 1:28) reminds us that even as we are in the awe-inspiring presence of God who sits on a judgment throne (see the mention of lightning and thunder – 5), we are also in the presence of the one who keeps his promises of mercy to his people and who will not again destroy his whole creation by water.

Twenty-four elders, perhaps representing the patriarchs and the apostles (21:12,14; see Isa 24:23), are worshipping God by throwing down their own crowns (4,10), and giving all glory to him alone. The whole impression is one of ceaseless praise before the throne (9). Four 'living creatures' (AV 'beasts') also worship. Again Ezekiel (1:10) saw something similar. It is because God is the creator that he deserves the worship of *all* his creatures (11). The lion is the greatest of the animal kingdom, the ox the greatest of the domestic animals, the eagle the greatest of birds and, of course, there is man. All are there because they were created 'by God's will' and for this very purpose of bringing glory to him.

With this view of God on his throne the song of praise must inevitably reflect on the holiness of God. God is not like his creatures, he is separate from them – part of the original meaning of 'holy'. The praise also reflects again the utter security for God's creatures, knowing that he 'was and is and is to come'.

5:1–14 The Lamb

This chapter introduces us to the scroll with seven seals. The opening of these seals one by one is the subject of the remainder of this vision through to chapter 8. The message that is revealed seems to centre largely on judgment but it also brings news of salvation. So what is the scroll? It is God's full purposes for the world and the fulfilment of history. The fact that it was written on both sides probably points to its completeness, and reminds us of a legal testament revealing details of the inheritance to be given out.

Perhaps it included the law of the Old Testament and the interpretation of the law that came through the prophets. Isaiah had spoken of the inability of people in his age to see God's will. To them it was 'like the words of a book that is sealed' (Isa 29:11), and he had prophesied of a day when the 'deaf shall hear the words of a book' (29:18). Christ is the one who brings the law and the prophets to fulfilment, and is therefore the only one who can open the scroll and show what will happen as God's will is carried out. Christ is the 'executor' of this testament or legal document. Adam had refused to carry out the will of God back in the Garden of Eden and had not taken the inheritance that God offered, but here in the scroll are the details of the inheritance. Is it any wonder that John weeps when no one can be found to open it? No one is worthy because, following Adam, no one has been fully obedient to its contents.

But there *is* one man who is worthy: the Lamb. Notice the great description of Jesus: he is both Messiah and conqueror (Lion, Root of David, 5), and also the Lamb (5). Try to picture what John describes. It is the victorious Messiah who is to open the scroll and he '*has conquered*' (past tense). He is responsible for sending out the Holy Spirit to the world ('the seven spirits', 6; John 15:26). He is already the victorious King. How? Well, John looks up and sees a Lamb that had been killed! This is the mystery of the incarnation. In dying on the cross Christ has become the perfectly obedient, suffering servant of Isaiah 53. As the one who has conquered sin, he is given the scroll by God the Father (7). The Lamb reminds us of the Passover lambs slaughtered when God redeemed his people from Israel (Exod 12:5–6,13). This is the picture that was taken up by John the Baptist in his description of Jesus (John 1:29), and it is this understanding of Jesus as Lamb that will remain prominent through the book of Revelation.

The remainder of the chapter describes the praise that Jesus receives. There are three hymns of praise sung by different groups: 9–10, 11–12, 13–14.

As we stand in the presence of the victorious Lamb all the redemptive purposes of God are revealed. Just as chapter 4 led us to worship the Father, so here we find the only possible response is to worship his Son, the Lamb.

An introduction to the visions of wrath

Chapters 4 and 5 have set a framework for the destruction that is going to dominate the visions in chapters 6–20. God has created (ch 4) and is to be worshipped. Jesus is victorious and has suffered to redeem fallen men and women and so is to be worshipped. This is a background of the marvellous graciousness of God in his workings with men and women and it must not be forgotten now as we see 'the wrath of the Lamb' (6:16).

Three main visions follow:

1. the breaking of seven seals;
2. the seven trumpets;
3. the seven bowls of wrath.

Each, in different ways, seems to describe similar things. There is great debate about the precise meaning of aspects of these visions, but it is best to start by reminding ourselves of some basic teaching in the Bible about the time that culminates in the second coming. We live in 'the last days', which are the days between Christ's first and second coming. Many parts of both Old and New Testaments indicate that during this period the elect will suffer, and the world will see considerable trials and tribulations. Some of those prophecies do not seem to have any particular time in mind during that period, while others possibly indicate that there will be an increase of trials towards the end, perhaps with one period of intense tribulation immediately before the Lord's return.

As we might expect in the picture we are given here, with the opening of each seal there is a distinct feeling that we are getting nearer to the final judgment day or second coming. 'Come!' (ch 6), repeated by each of the four living creatures, is the cry echoed down through the ages by the church pleading for the Lord's return (1 Cor 16:22; Rev 22:17,20). The four creatures represent the whole of the created order, which is involved in this cry of the church (compare Rom 8:22–23). The breaking of each seal brings that day closer.

The opening of the seventh seal reveals the book itself in which more details of God's judgment are given through further visions.

The successive disclosures closely parallel the words of Jesus in Mark 13:7–27, where the last days are indicated by the appearance of false christs, wars, earthquakes, famines, general persecution of Christians, darkening of the sun, stars falling and the shaking of powers in heaven, and the coming of Christ.

The background for the four horsemen revealed by the first four seals is found in Zechariah 1:8–17 and 6:1–8, where these are used as God's instruments to bring judgment on his people's enemies. The colours (Zech 6:6) stand for the four points of the compass, and it is likely that the same idea is present in Revelation 6. The whole earth is subject to this judgment.

6:1–17 The seals

The first seal is broken to reveal a white horse, and a rider with a crown. Some suggest that this is Jesus and the victory he brings (see Rev 19:11). Jesus thus heads the judgment while the other riders execute his will.

In the light of Mark 13, however, it is suggested that this horseman, like the rest, in fact brings evil. He cannot be Jesus, for it is Jesus who is opening the seals. Rather, here is a false christ or antichrist, and this explains the similarity between this rider and Christ in Revelation 19. This would parallel the list in Mark 13 of things to be encountered before the end. This second suggestion is probably the best.

The second horseman takes peace from the world. What a vivid thought to those who were being asked to endure even to death (2:10). The third brings economic hardship, already being experienced by some of the churches (2:9). The fourth brings death, famine and pestilence, as God's judgment courses through the world. The seven churches are already tasting it.

The fifth seal shows the saints 'under the altar'. This is a description of the fact that they had died for the faith. This is no easy time for Christians. Many have been martyred and await vengeance which, rightly, they have left in the hands of God (Rom 12:19).

The sixth scene would be particularly appropriate to people who had recently experienced dreadful earthquakes. It is a regularly occurring picture of the wrath of God (eg Mark 13:24–25; Ezek 32:7–8), and seems to sum up all the previous statements. This is a time of devastation for all.

By this stage things are so bad that people will recognize they are experiencing 'the wrath of the Lamb'. Unbelievers will arrogantly say that no one can stand (survive) before the wrath. This is what they have always claimed, that the faith of the Christian is in vain. Not so; believers will be safe (7:4). The surviving unbelievers fail to take this opportunity to repent (9:20).

Some of what we experience in today's church is similar to what is described as the seals are opened. Parts of the church are fiercely persecuted, others suffer famine, or economic hardship, or are caught up in war. If we fail to recognize this as a description of our own church then we have failed to recognize the truth of Scripture that when one part of the body suffers, all suffer (1 Cor 12:26). These are pointers that we are indeed in the last days, just as they were for the seven churches who must have related so personally to the message. It may well be that things have yet to get much, much worse. But the coming of the Lord will be like a 'thief' in the night (3:3). We need to be aware that the things revealed by the seals are released under Christ's authority and will divide believers from unbelievers. Are we prepared?

7:1–8 The seal of the
living God

Now we await the opening of the final seal and the completion of God's purposes. But the question of 6:17 must first be answered, and the answer is here in verse 4. Those sealed by God are the ones who are able to stand. The judgment is held in check while the elect are sealed. This idea recalls the blood of the Passover lamb that sealed the children of Israel against the judgment on Egypt.

As the image of destruction now changes to four winds, we have a further indication that we must be very careful indeed not to look for precise literal equivalents of everything we read in this letter. The nature of the imagery being used is flexible. After all, it is only with flexible, moving imagery that humans could ever hope to describe the final purposes of God. The four winds stand for the destruction that occurs on the earth in the later visions of the trumpets and bowls (see Zech 6:5).

There is discussion about the identity of the 144,000. Some suggest that they represent the remnant of physical Israel, that is, faithful Jews. In our view it is more likely that they represent the church. For the New Testament writers, the concept of a distinction between Jew and Gentile had been challenged: all are one in Christ. The promises once thought to apply only to physical Israel have been shown to apply to all Christians. A 'real' Jew is one 'inwardly' said Paul (Rom 2:28–29; see Rev 2:9; 3:9), and he even called the church 'the Israel of God' (Gal 6:16). Here in Revelation itself it is Christians as a whole who are called by the old Jewish term: a kingdom of priests (1:6; 5:10; Exod 19:6).

The figure of 144,000 is symbolic of completeness (note the use of multiples of twelve for this purpose, eg 21:12,14,16; 22:2). The mention of the twelve tribes also indicates the complete universality of the elect.

This is a chapter of joy for its speaks of the security that the elect will have in spite of the coming of judgment. To the seven churches such assurance would be vital as they realized that things might get worse, and some of them might have to die for their faith and suffer in the natural catastrophes brought by the wrath of the Lamb.

But this book is not just for them. It is a comfort to all God's people right through the ages until Christ returns, that he will never let them go, but will protect them and lead them safely through these events. Even if things do get worse for Christians during an exceptional period of 'tribulation' towards the end (see next section), yet still our Sovereign Lord has sealed us for his own. We belong to him and his word is our assurance and our confidence. We need not be fearful for our salvation. Heaven awaits us.

Questions for further study and discussion on Revelation 1–7:8

1. What is John writing in this book, and to whom? What does he have in common with these people? Jesus is in the midst of today's lampstands. What do you think he finds that most saddens him?

2. Has your 'first love' faded? What can you 'remember' that will re-kindle that love? Of what should you repent? What works should you now be doing?

3. Do you believe your church is guilty of a wrong sort of accommodation to the world? What responsibility do you as an individual have in this? In what ways do you individually take on board in your thinking the world's ideas and values?

4. The church at Sardis seems to have moved away from the truth in its practice of Christianity. Do you and do others think of your church as 'alive'? Is it really alive? If not, what can you do about it?

5. What is the purpose of trials? What should our attitude be to them?

6. Can you think of any ways in which you have personally closed a door on Jesus? Has this happened in the life of your local church (3:20)?

7. Look carefully at chapter 4 and list at least *five* reasons for praising God.

8. Why is Christ the Lamb praised in chapter 5? How might we praise him better?

9. What indications (local, national, international) are there that you live in the last days?

10. What difference does it make to you as a Christian that you are 'sealed'? Think of something you are experiencing in your life at the moment where the joy of this truth will help you.

7:9–17 A great multitude

Having *heard* (3) of the sealing of Christians, John now *sees* beyond the time of wrath and tribulation into heaven itself. A great multitude of people from the whole world are worshipping God. They have indeed been kept for the time when they will experience the glory of heaven and be in the presence of God and the Lamb. The vision breaks into the most wonderful description of the privileges of the saints who know the Lamb, not as the one who brings wrath, but as the one who will be their shepherd!

The fact that these people have white robes and have 'come out of the great tribulation' has caused problems concerning their identity. Some have suggested that these are the final number of martyrs anticipated by the opening of the fifth seal (6:9–11). The great tribulation, it is said, is a period of particular persecution that breaks out just before the coming of Christ (see on 3:10; Dan 12:1). This is possible, and yet the passage as a whole makes us think of something more general. These are the company of all believers, for all believers have been sealed. We actually catch a glimpse here of ourselves in the future. We will be in that company if we are called and sealed, if we believe in Christ Jesus. Great tribulation may refer to a special time of crisis, yet suffering in varying degrees is to be the lot of all God's people (1:9; Acts 14:22; see 1 Cor 12:26).

As the pictures of wrath and affliction build up over the next few chapters we now have three important truths to keep in mind.

1. God is sovereign and seated on the throne in heaven where he is worshipped for ever (chapter 4; 7:10–12).

2. The Lamb brings God's plans to fulfilment, and receives the same praise as the Father. He has redeemed men and women by his death; he now has all power and authority, and is worshipped for ever (chapter 5; 7:10,17).

3. The living God seals those who belong to the Lamb so that, come what may, they will join that great body of praise in heaven.

These truths must be borne in mind, for without them we would be confronted with despair and hopelessness in the face of tribulation and wrath. It is hard for those of us who have never personally experienced severe affliction to picture this wonderful glory. Perhaps therefore we should try to imagine the severest persecutions of our fellow Christians today, in countries around the world, and then contrast the extreme pain, the tears, the rags and torn clothing, the blood and the death with the 'shelter' of God's presence (15) – no hunger, nor tears, nor thirst, nor scorching sun but rather white robes and a shepherd leading to springs of living water! With this in store, no wonder the cry of the saints down the ages has been 'Come, Lord!'

8:1–12 Seven trumpets

John's vision now returns us to the opening of the seals. With the seventh seal we expect to see the final judgment, and yet we are given a dramatic picture in which everything stops in heaven while God receives the prayers of his saints. The importance of prayer is at once seen. The saints are praying for justice to be done and for Christ to 'Come' (6:10; Luke 18:7).

The church often fails in this aspect of prayer. To pray for Christ to come must include prayer for the Lord's name to be upheld in the judgment of all those who have stood against him and his people. Christians are so afraid of judgment these days that they would often rather forget its existence. But it is our duty to be concerned with the Lord's justice both in judgment as well as in salvation. In our prayers we must ask that God will defend utter holiness and justice. Praying 'thy kingdom come' is asking God to come in judgment on evil, not just that he speed the day of our final salvation.

Through the imagery of incense and the temple we see prayers rising into the very presence of God. There they are mixed with the prayers of all who already worship in his presence. Seven angels, the agents of the wrath of the Lamb, wait with trumpets for his command.

This is the land of visions and prophecy. Chronological order is not clear and the visions of wrath overlap considerably in their descriptions. It is possible that the trumpets reveal different aspects of the *same* series of judgments as were released by the breaking of the seals. Some have said the seals concentrate on judgment on the whole world, while the trumpets view the proceedings from the perspective of the unbeliever. This is certainly possible.

The trumpets announce the day of the Lord (Matt 24:31). The first four blasts describe destruction on the world around us. Many of these images find their background in the Old Testament, especially in the plagues that came on Egypt and in the prophetic descriptions of judgment to be found in the Prophets (see, for instance, Amos 5:18; 7:17–8:12).

The Old Testament understanding that the first-born son inherits a double portion may explain why only one-third of things is destroyed. The two-thirds may be held back to symbolize the inheritance that belongs to the sons of God. Others suggest that the final judgment still has not come and that time is being given for repentance. But 9:20 seems to make this less likely.

We have begun to taste more deeply the wrath of God (7–12) and it is horrific to us. We shall be preserved through this, but it must affect us as we pray for the speedy return of Christ, and for the salvation of those around us who are rebelling against the Lord. Do we ever pray 'How long, O Lord?' as we see the evil in our world? One day we will see God's justice prevail fully.

8:13–9:12 Apollyon

This section is introduced by the announcement of a 'Woe' (8:13) to those 'who dwell on the earth': unbelievers (see on 3:10). There are to be three woes (9:12), the second is probably linked to the sixth trumpet and the third to the descent of Satan in 12:12. The eagle may be a destroying vulture (Hos 8:1; Matt 24:28).

Satan, for that is whom the fallen star would appear to represent (see Luke 10:18), is given great power here over the world. But we should note that this is delegated power. He can only do what God allows him to do: 'he was given the key . . .' (1), 'they were told . . .' (4), 'they were allowed . . .' (5). This is very important for, while there is little joy to be drawn from this intensely tragic passage, we can still see the sovereignty of God being maintained over the earth. Satan has no power over those who are sealed (4). God keeps his word to his elect even as the judgment happens all around them.

Paul knew of the truth underlying this passage when he wrote Romans 8:28–39. Not even the very worst tribulation can separate Christians from the love of God. At a yet deeper level Paul knew that God's plan is so sure that even evil itself is made to serve his purposes. Nowhere can the truth of this be seen more clearly than in this part of John's vision. Here Satan is allowed great power by God, and the end result is that he (Satan) brings *God*'s judgment on his own evil followers!

Satan hopes to bring terror to believers, yet he only succeeds in causing his own people to suffer so much that they want to die. The description of torture need not be taken literally to the extent that we expect plagues of scorpions, but it would be wrong to weaken the effect of this imagery. Satan brings continuous pain to this world. Paul has also described how physical suffering follows from sin (Rom 1:24–32).

This is the world we live in and Satan is alive and active. We see people around us caught up in the pain and suffering of their own sin. The work Satan has started in their lives leads to their suffering. Adultery leads to the pain of broken families; lying and cheating lead to some of the widespread feelings of insecurity we so often meet. We cannot say we sympathize with such people's sufferings if we do not also point them to the cause. To try to deal with the symptoms without pointing to the personal reality of Satan is to deceive people and further the work of the enemy.

Even many church leaders in our day refuse to acknowledge the reality of Satan. There can be little more satisfying to him than to know that some people will read this fearful description and yet continue to deny his existence. He is truly Apollyon: the Destroyer.

9:13–21 No repentance

Just as with the sixth seal, when people remain totally arrogant in their sin even in the midst of the wrath of God, and would rather the rocks fall on them than have to seek mercy, so here, as plagues are released in judgment on sinful people, there is still no repentance from the ones who survive.

It is an indication of how hardened people can become in their sin that, having just witnessed the power of the true God, revealed in judgment, they turn back to worship their man-made gods. What they have witnessed is the most terrible of judgments, and they now only await the seventh trumpet and the coming of Christ himself. They have seen a third of men die.

The Euphrates, often mentioned in the Old Testament, was the area from which the great invading, killing and plundering forces came against Israel. Here is a picture of invading forces, like the Assyrians and Babylonians, that bring death. In the Old Testament both these nations were understood to bring God's judgment on the unbelieving people of Israel. The numbers of the army are, of course, far too massive to be envisaged in literal terms, even in the twentieth century. Rather this continues to be a description of demonic forces at work in the world, hence their horses with 'lion's heads' with 'tails like serpents'. John's vision is of the destruction that comes on all evil people.

We have suggested that these symbolic descriptions can apply to any age as we continue to live in the last days. It is wrong to deduce that we definitely live in the generation in which Christ will return. But the sixth trumpet may be a forceful reminder to us, living in a nuclear age, and to a generation that has seen millions and millions killed in two world wars, that God continues to judge this world. We can see it happening around us. We await Christ's return with eagerness so that this devastating period of history may be left behind and God may be acknowledged as just and righteous.

The opening letters to the seven churches warned Christians of God's judgment on those who followed immorality and idolatry (2:14–16,20–23). Though we noted that those letters were for all the churches, the specific mention of immorality, idolatry and so on in 20–21 must have been a particularly powerful message for Thyatira. Here is a warning again to Christians that we should make sure we *do* belong to the Lord and are sealed, or are we simply deceiving ourselves as the great deceiver would desire? Idols made of silver may seem remote to us, but murder, sorcery, immorality and theft might be a summary of the six o'clock news!

10:1–11 The little scroll

Chapters 10:1–11:13 form another interlude not unlike that found in chapter 7 where the saints were sealed. We still await the last trumpet. The scene of the vision now changes to earth (1). Again we must accept the ebb and flow of the visionary perceptions in this sort of literature. We are not given an explanation for the change of scene.

A mighty angel brings the message, and the description of this being impresses upon us his glory. The picture of v 2 does not indicate the angel's size so much as the fact that what he has to say involves the whole world. The rainbow reminds us that the message is part of the total fulfilment of God's covenantal plans for his people.

Next we learn of the speaking of 'the seven thunders'. This probably refers to God himself (see Ps 29:3) but, tantalizingly, what was spoken remains personal to John for he is not allowed to reveal it to us (see 2 Cor 12:4 where Paul also heard what could not be repeated). The angel then goes on to say that there should be 'no more delay' (6). This looks forward to the sounding of the seventh trumpet (11:15–19). There comes a time, which John now witnesses, when God will no longer delay in bringing his final judgment day to the world. There has been time for the sealing of the saints, there has been time for repentance, but eventually the great Day is coming.

However, John's part in this whole process must first be established, for this chapter is in part his private experience. He is to absorb fully the message of God as a prophet in this last age. Here we are reminded of Ezekiel who also ate a scroll (Ezek 2:9–3:3). John's scroll was bitter and sweet. His is the privileged calling to be a prophet in the last days. The message of the coming of Christ and the fulfilment of all the Old Testament prophecies is sweet. But the message is also bitter, for along with the covenant blessings of Christ's second coming come all the horrors of the judgment and wrath and covenant curses on those who have not repented. John's task will be to prophesy about the events heralded by the seventh trumpet. His message will be for 'many peoples' (11) and we shall have to listen carefully.

While we await the seventh trumpet it is worth remembering that, though we are not called to be prophets in the way John was, we *are* called to proclaim the truth of the gospel, which includes this message from John. It would sometimes appear that we think of it only as sweet. If we have really absorbed the truth of the gospel and the meaning of the return of Christ then we too will realize that part of that message is bitter to the stomach for it involves proclaiming the judgment of God on sinful people.

11:1–14 Two prophetic witnesses

There is no doubt that this is one of the most difficult parts of John's book to interpret. But first it is worth noting that this section and ch 10 are connected with the sixth trumpet blast and the second woe (9:12–13; see 11:14). The problem that faces us is how to interpret the references to the temple, altar and to the holy city (1–2).

1. Some have said that this passage deals with the place of the Jewish people in the last days, and that this is a prophecy of a time when the temple has been rebuilt and the Jews will face the antichrist. The temple, altar and city are thus to be taken literally.

2. Another view takes the passage symbolically but still as referring to the way in which God will ultimately look after the Jewish people. Jerusalem represents the Jewish people. The temple is 'measured', symbolizing their being set apart for preservation by God (see Zech 2:1–5). The fact that only the central part of the temple is measured indicates that only a remnant of Jews will be saved.

3. Others regard this whole section as referring symbolically to the church, which can be called the 'temple of God' (1 Cor 3:16). Jerusalem and the outer courts are symbolic of the 'nations'. Thus there is a parallel in this passage with the sealing of the saints in ch 7. Here the church (the temple) is measured for protection. But it will still suffer at the hands of the nations. This view, it is said, brings ch 11 more into line with the thought of ch 10 and shows that it is following the ideas seen under the previous visions where the church suffers but is protected.

In order to benefit from the teaching of this chapter a decision on these matters is necessary. This is not easy and each position has strong arguments in its favour. We take the passage as most likely referring to the church because of the surrounding context which has distinguished between the church and the world. The preceding symbolism strongly suggests that the whole picture here is also to be regarded symbolically (see esp. 8 where this is explicit). On the meanings of the times mentioned, see the Further Notes on the next page.

We therefore understand this passage to be a prophecy telling how the church will bear faithful witness even while all around is in the hand of the enemy. God will protect this witness. Two witnesses (see Further Notes) are mentioned perhaps because witness borne by two people stands for that which is completely true (Deut 17:6; John 8:17). A time of dreadful persecution comes on the church, but still God raises it up and the great reward of heaven is awaiting (12). What joy that even as the church witnesses and is persecuted (2:10) God remains sovereign, and the great hope of the resurrection remains!

Further notes on 11:1–14

Times

Undoubtedly the references in Revelation to specific periods of time are difficult to understand. Are they to be taken literally? Are they some kind of symbol? If they are symbolic, is there any key available to help us understand the meanings, or do they have to remain enigmatic in this age?

Before we attempt an answer to this we should note:

1. Some of the numbers are repeated in different ways. Forty-two months (a month = 30 days), mentioned in 11:2 and 13:5, is the same period of time as 1260 days (11:3; 12:6). This, of course, is three and a half years. Now in Daniel 7:25 and 12:7, we read of 'a time, two times, and half a time'. If a 'time' is a year, then again we have three and a half years. This idea is explicitly picked up in Revelation 12:14.

2. Whether or not we take this literally, the background for the idea can be seen in the Old Testament in Daniel. There in chapter 7 we read of the power and rule for this limited time of the 'beast' – a figure introduced to us in Revelation 11:7 as the one who comes up from the bottomless pit.

The nations will trample over the holy city for the three and a half years, which is the time of the beast's authority (see 13:5–17), the length of time in which the witnesses prophesy (11:3) and the length of time for which the woman (church) will be 'nourished' in the wilderness (12:6). The three and a half days (11:9,11) perhaps reminds us of Jesus' own experience of suffering, the cross and the resurrection. Certainly it is thus possible to see these numbers symbolically, especially if it is remembered that the number seven is always considered to be a perfect number. Three and a half, being half of fulness or perfection may indicate, therefore, the fact that all this still remains firmly in God's control and that he will bring it to conclusion. The consummation has yet to come, but it will come. Meanwhile, the troubles are for a limited period of time and under the sovereign control of the only one who brings all things to completion.

The witnesses

The two witnesses probably stand symbolically for the truth of the witness of the church. After all, their death is seen by people throughout the whole world (9), and it is unlikely that 'war' would be waged simply on two individuals (7). Also 'lampstands' (4) reminds us of the churches called 'lampstands' in chs 1 and 2. But we should also note the links that John makes between them and Moses and Elijah. Elijah 'shut the sky' to rain and Moses turned waters into blood and smote the earth with plagues (1 Kings 17:1; Exod 7:14–24). Therefore some have said that as John the Baptist was the embodiment of Elijah, so two great prophets (the embodiment of Moses and Elijah) will arise to usher in the final days.

11:15–19 The seventh trumpet and the kingdom of God

With the seventh trumpet we expect either the end to come immediately or the third woe, but neither takes place. Instead 'the days' (10:7) in which both events happen are introduced. Still to follow are many other visions of coming events. However, in these few verses we are given a clear foresight of that final day when 'the kingdom of the world has become the kingdom of our Lord and of his Christ'. John transports us to a time when Jesus is worshipped as the one who was and who is (17), but no longer 'to come', for now his kingdom has arrived.

This section seems to give us in summary all that we are to see through the second half of the book. It concentrates on a scene to which John will not return until chapters 21–22, but gives a glorious preview.

Throughout history men and women of faith have talked of their expectation of the great day when they will see Christ coming in glory. It is worth pausing to meditate on verses 15–17 for so often in these days we seem to lose sight of this glorious time.

John shows that Psalm 2 prophesied about these events. There we see the nations (Ps 2:1) plotting against God's people, the kings of the earth setting themselves against his anointed. But now the 'kingdom of the earth' is replaced by the 'kingdom of our Lord'. John is not saying that God was not king before this time, for he is sovereign over the whole universe all through history and is the only Lord. Never before, however, have the nations of the earth had to acknowledge that fact. They have deliberately turned against the truth, and now they can do so no longer. As Caird (p 141) says: 'A king may be king *de jure*, but he is not king *de facto* until the trumpet which announces his accession is answered by the acclamations of a loyal and obedient people'. The faithful Christians through the ages and the believers of the Old Testament have always acknowledged that kingship. On the last day no one will be able to deny it.

The king brings with him judgment that carries wrath and rewards. The suffering elect, and especially the martyrs, will have nothing to fear, but rather much in which to rejoice as at last the cry 'How long?' (6:10) is answered.

Again we are reminded that true desire for Christ to return is also a desire that judgment should come on the world. There is nothing shameful in this. We should always want to see the righteousness and justice of the Lord being upheld. It should be one of our greatest desires to see evil finally banished and the Lord acknowledged throughout the world.

12:1–17 The woman and the child

Christians enter the kingdom of God 'through many tribulations' (Acts 14:22). Chapters 12 to 14 help us to understand why and how these things happen. Here is a panoramic picture of the great fight through history between the people of God and Satan: an idea that dominates much of the book. The church must take encouragement from these chapters as the Lamb triumphs and judges.

1. *The Woman.* The woman is not necessarily Mary about to bear Christ, as some suggest, but more probably the true Israel in every age – the elect people of God. Certainly the reference is to the one who bore the Messiah but, as in Isaiah 9:6–7, 26:17–18, 66:7–8 and Micah 5:2–3, it is likely that the idea is that the whole community of the faithful has struggled in giving birth. The passage is talking about the ongoing persecution of the elect people, the church of God. Her bright and glorious clothes emphasize strongly the contrast between her and the prostitute of ch 17.

2. *The Child.* Psalm 2 is used again and reveals clearly that the child is Christ (5). Even when Satan thought that he was finally about to capture the Messiah for ever, Christ was 'caught up to God' (the resurrection and ascension). The description of the fight in heaven which follows, shows that Christ defeats Satan. Although Michael is mentioned, the song of praise (10–12a) indicates that it is Christ's death which makes this possible. So, in a vivid description (7–13) of the forces of God (Michael and his angels) winning a battle against the forces of evil, we discover why the dragon has set himself so strongly against the woman: he has already been defeated. The child is on the throne (5), and we have learnt that the real battle is not between the forces of good and the forces of evil in general, but between Christ and Satan, and Christ is the victor.

3. *The Dragon.* Satan, the red dragon (3, also called the serpent 14–17), has considerable authority and power, signified by the diadems, the tail and the horns. (See Dan 7:7,24.) However, just as Israel was delivered from Egypt, so the woman is kept safe in the wilderness. The wilderness is a symbol for the safe-keeping of God's people (see Exod 19:1–4). The example of the wilderness continues with the idea that Satan's efforts to destroy the church are 'swallowed up' by the earth (see Exod 15:12; Isa 43:2; 50:2).

What wonder and joy for those of us today, who are part of this great and everlasting church of God, to know that while Satan is still doing his very best to destroy us, the battle is already won in heaven. The child is Lord, and we too share in the victory as Christ continually protects us. It is just as Jesus has told us in John 10:28 speaking of his people as 'sheep': 'No one shall snatch them out of my hand'.

13:1–10 The worship of a parody of Christ

Satan's attack on the 'offspring' of the woman is the final desperate fling of a defeated being. The theme of chapter 12 continues.

We were introduced to the beast in 11:7. This figure is drawn from Daniel. The beast John sees seems to epitomize all the horrors of the four beasts mentioned in Daniel 7:3–8. In Revelation 14 when John moves on to looking at how the saints will survive, he returns again to Daniel 7 and the victory that comes with the son of man (Rev 14:14; Dan 7:13). 19:19 pictures for us a uniting of the beast and the kings of the earth before finally he is defeated and thrown into the lake of fire. Between chapters 11 and 19, however, the figure of the beast (or beasts as in this chapter) is prominent as an agent for the work of Satan. But who is the beast?

Some suggest that mention of a head with a mortal wound that was healed refers to the Emperor Nero (see Introduction), who was said to have come alive after his death. A myth like this would have made such a vision especially relevant to the Christians of John's day. How easily they would be able to identify the beast with the Roman emperors who were setting themselves up as God. But, primarily, it seems that John is reminded in his vision of Genesis 3:15. Revelation 12:17 showed us that the dragon was chasing the offspring. Having the mortal wound shows that Satan has been defeated, and yet he is permitted by God to live on for a while. The curse on Satan in the Garden of Eden is finally coming to fulfilment. Satan will not be able to do anything more than 'bruise the heel' of God's people.

Everything about the beast, his assumed authority, and even his apparent resurrection, is a parody of the true Christ. The beast is not simply Nero, nor is he simply a symbol of some great manifestation of the antichrist at the very end of time. Nero, Rome, Nazi Germany and so on, are all continuing examples of this work of the beast. As men abuse power and government and assume to themselves rights that belong only to God, so the monster in fact becomes the state – given over completely to the power of Satan. Institutionalized persecution of Christians becomes the norm. We should be aware that the beast is with us right now. Humanism has virtually complete control in our society. Man sets up his own structures and laws. The usurping of God's position is blasphemy (5–6).

If it were not for the fact that we are utterly secure with our names in the Lamb's book of life (8), then we too would find ourselves worshipping the beast. How easily we are led astray into thinking that this is not relevant to us! We think of governments elsewhere in the world, but what of our own situation, and how much have we been prepared to compromise as our minds have been saturated with the philosophy of the Enemy?

13:11–18 A false prophet

The beast from the sea, although not called the 'antichrist', parodied Christ. This second beast arises from the earth and is to be identified with a 'false prophet' (16:13; 19:20; 20:10). He is to bring glory to the first beast and make the people of earth worship him (12). He performs signs, and with his *two* horns (11) he parodies the true witness (11:3) and deceives people.

As with the first beast, it is suggested that this figure refers to some unique power or person appearing with the antichrist at the end of history. While we have agreed that this may be possible, we have suggested that it is more likely that the whole period of 'the last days' is in view, from Christ's first coming to his second. We have acknowledged that it is possible that things will get substantially worse just before Christ returns (although the evidence is not overwhelming for this position) but, even here, such a view does not adequately do justice to what John is saying. In the Introduction it was stressed that what John wrote had direct relevance for the seven churches, but so it has for us today. It is perhaps best to understand the beast as continuing to fight God's people from the death of Christ until his return.

Taking this view, the main problem in these verses is the enigmatic reference to the 'mark' of 666. If this is a literal mark then clearly it is not visible on people at the moment. This has given rise to so much speculation we cannot possibly deal with it all here. Suffice it to say that it does not refer to the sort of tattoo-figure seen on evil people in modern occult-type films, nor does it refer to the ubiquitous numbers found on credit cards! It is just possible that the numbers are equal to a name, since numbers can occasionally stand for letters. Thus some say it may signify 'Nero Caesar'. However, John elsewhere uses numbers symbolically, not as direct equivalents. We know that seven is the number of fulness or perfection, and it is a divine number. Perhaps therefore we may see 666, a 'human number' (18), as never perfect but always imperfect, symbolizing the epitome of evil.

Jesus had spoken of false prophets and false christs. This chapter has described both. The danger to our generation, which longs to see 'signs and wonders', is enormous. We are easily led astray by anything that seems remotely abnormal. We are far too quick to attribute everything to God. John warns us in 1 John 4:1 not to believe every spirit. He tells us that the antichrists have come and that it is the last hour (1 John 2:18). How prepared are we? Are we also sucked into the worship of the beast because of our fascination with the spectacular, our materialistic desire for money and health? The influence of humanistic materialism is seen in the way that we are prepared to tolerate false teaching and prophecy in our churches.

Questions for further study and discussion on Revelation 7:9–13:18

1. Think of those Christians who are persecuted in the world today. Pray for them. Does your prayer reflect the desire for the Lord's return?

2. How seriously do you take the need to pray for God to come and vindicate us, his saints?

3. In what ways might a deeper understanding of the activity of Satan in this world affect our evangelism among non-Christians? What practical difference does it make to us to know that Satan's power is limited by God?

4. Do you see evidence around you of the world's hardness of heart? How might what we call 'natural disasters' be accounted for in the light of 9:17–19? How do they fit into the total picture of God's sovereignty as shown thus far in this book?

5. In reading the passage about the 'little scroll' our attention is again drawn to the whole message of the gospel (see question 3 above). Why is the 'bitter' part of the message so difficult for us to handle? How would you present the full gospel message if you had half an hour with a non-Christian, knowing that he or she was about to die?

6. In what ways is the church witnessing in this age? To what extent is it suffering as a result of its witness? Should it be stronger in its witness? If so, in what areas of life is there special need for consistent proclamation of truth?

7. Why is it important that Christ is *King*?

8. Do you *feel* like the woman kept safe in the wilderness, or are you tempted to forget the victory and protecting power of Christ?

9. How can we avoid being deceived by the beast? Is it inevitable that we too will worship the dragon?

10. Look again at the last paragraph of the comments on 13:11–18. Do you tolerate false teaching and prophecy? How do you know the difference between what is true and what is false?

14:1–5 The Lamb and the redeemed

In chapter 13 the triumph of the beasts and dragon seems almost complete. They have been allowed to 'conquer', that is to put to death, the saints (13:7,15). And yet the period of the dragon's power is limited (12:12) to the symbolic three and a half years (forty-two months – 13:5). This is the time during which the woman (the church) is nourished 'in the wilderness' (12:6,14).

Now John receives a vision of great encouragement. This is not a leap into the future; here we see the real position of the Lamb and of his people who are suffering at the hands of the beast. This is still part of the present context of the appeal for 'the endurance of the saints' (13:10; 14:12). The attacks of the beasts are in the present world, and the messages of the angels (14:6ff) are for this world. So is this vision.

The 144,000 (7:4) are the redeemed who belong to God (note the contrast between the mark on them and the mark on those who worship the beast). They do not worship the beast. And now they appear on Mount Zion with the Lamb. But to what does Mount Zion refer? It may simply be a symbol of the place of victory (Joel 2:32, Ps 2:6 – which may lie behind this whole section). Some say it refers to the time when Christ returns and establishes a millennial kingdom on earth, but we have suggested that the context is more concerned with current realities. Is it possible to conclude that John sees the same persecuted people with the Lamb in heaven even while they are being persecuted? Certainly this is possible. Paul speaks of the same thing when he says that God 'raised us up with [Christ], and made us sit with him in the heavenly places in Christ Jesus' (Eph 2:6). Even now Christians share in the rule of Christ. The wonderful truth is that we are 'in him' and totally secure. Verses 6–20 will show what should be proclaimed during this period of tribulation.

The great temptation for the church has always been twofold: **1.** to compromise with the world; and **2.** to become overly pietistic and opt out of the world, simply waiting and suffering until Christ returns to rescue. John has already shown that compromise is wrong. The second option is now also seen to be wrong. The church is not called to suffer passively, but to preach the gospel extrovertly and directly and to keep the commandments of God. The church is involved in warfare with the dragon. He wants everything to obey him. *We* must seek to bring *every* area of life in this world into obedience to Christ.

Note: 'Defiled ... with women', and being 'chaste' (4), has caused some interpreters problems. It is typical biblical metaphorical language for going after other gods. The redeemed are those who have not worshipped the beast – who have not gone after idols (Ezek 16:15–22; 1 Chron 5:25).

14:6–20 The gospel

While the vision in 14:1–5 has brought the wonderful truth to the saints of their position before God and with the Lamb even while they are suffering or being put to death here on earth, the next verses show that in spite of this the church is to continue to proclaim the gospel. Here the angels proclaim the message, but this task is also the 'deeds' and 'labour' of the saints.

No doubt the angels' messages come as a reminder to the saints of the gospel message in which they must believe and for which they must endure (12), but they also come as a message to the world. This eternal message of the gospel is the same that the church has proclaimed and must continue to proclaim while there is still any time at all for repentance. It is this message that will lead to direct persecution of the saints, and it will lead to many having to die, but still it must be told to the world. Once again it is likely that the words of Mark 13 are in mind, where Jesus spoke of the gospel being preached to all nations and of the persecution of believers (Mark 13:9–13 – note the need for endurance also mentioned in that passage).

Again the grace of God is seen in all its magnificence. Just when the dragon is seen to be at the height of his authority, and the church at its weakest, God still ensures that the gospel is heard in the world.

But why is this called a gospel message (6)? – after all, most of the angels' words concern judgment. How frequently we forget that the gospel actually looks forward to the coming judgment day. This is the time when God's final, sovereign power will be seen, and when the suffering church will be vindicated. But it is also the time when Satan will finally be completely defeated and sin will be eradicated. In all God's dealings with men and women, even back in the Old Testament covenants, two alternatives lie before them: blessing or curse. People may be recipients of the grace of God or, if they deliberately rebel and turn against him, they will be the recipients of his judgment (7; Gen 2:15–17; Deut 11:26–28; John 3:16–21). Babylon, that is, the evil world set against God, *will* fall (8). The seven churches would probably have recognized Babylon in terms of Rome and the empire (see the reference to the 'seven mountains', 17:4–7,9,18).

Jesus himself comes to judge the earth. The picture used of a 'son of man' comes from Daniel 7. The cloud indicates the full, pervasive presence of God in this final act in the history of the present world. The coming of Christ is the exciting climax of history for the suffering church (13), yet it is full of dreadful horror for those who have persistently rejected God (9–10).

How does the gospel message that we proclaim today match up to the fulness of the gospel message as seen in this passage? Perhaps we might be more eager to see people saved if from time to time we re-read verses 17–20.

Summary

We can summarize the situation described in the last few chapters like this: the church is a faithful witness to God (ch 11), but is severely persecuted by the dragon (Satan), who seeks to destroy it because he has been thrown out of heaven by the child. The child is the Christ, who is now Lord (ch 12). On earth, in the limited time at his disposal before God's final and complete judgment takes place, Satan therefore seeks to do his worst to the saints. Through deception in the form of a false christ (13:1–8) and a false prophet (13:11–18), he nearly succeeds in his task. Saints are put to death, and Satan would indeed completely conquer except that the saints are sealed (7:1–8), and have their names in the book of life (13:8).

While this persecution goes on, however, Christians should remember that the Lamb is sovereign, and should draw comfort from the fact that the eternal realities are such that they already rule with Christ because they are redeemed (14:1–5).

The visions of the angels remind us that the last days are here and that, just as Jesus commanded (Mark 13), the gospel must be proclaimed to every nation. The gospel brings the promise of life, and a call for endurance to the saints, but fearful consequences for those who persist in following the beast and turning their backs on the Lamb (14:6–20). For those who die while labouring for the Lord, there is special encouragement. Once again, Satan appears to have won by causing the death of some of the children of God but, in fact, it is seen that God has conquered and what Satan meant for their hurt, God uses to their eternal blessing (14:13).

Now the vision moves on to the outpouring of the 'seven bowls of the wrath of God' (ch 16). This may be a description of the 'third woe' mentioned in 11:14 as coming soon.

15:1–8 Joy in heaven

Already John has shown us visions of God's judgments on earth in many different ways, but primarily through the seven seals and the seven trumpets. Now he sees seven bowls of the wrath of God. (As the vision progresses it becomes clear that the plagues and the bowls are identical.) It may sound strange to our ears that, as these angels are seen, John also sees a great body of people praising the Lamb for his judgments. But we must remember what we have already read, and we must try to remove ourselves from our own framework of twentieth-century compromise into this biblical perspective.

We await the fulfilment of God's purposes if we are truly his people. We know that those purposes include the most precious blessings for the children of God, but they also include wrath for those who have the mark of the beast. We have already seen how the prayers of the saints are involved in bringing about God's righteous judgment (8:3–5). But we have also noted that the martyrs do right in praying that the Lord will avenge them (6:9–11). If we understand the great horror of the power of evil, then we should not seek to excuse it; we should pray that God's perfect justice and judgment will be seen.

Note how two songs are sung. Perhaps they are welded in one, for obviously the idea is that the faithful of the Old Testament era are joining with the faithful of the New Testament era to sing God's great praise. The covenant promises and curses are coming to fulfilment. How difficult this is for us! We want the friendship and love of Christ without a proper understanding of the holiness of God. This chapter keeps reminding us of the holiness of God (esp. v 8) – not just as morally upright, but as awesomely separate from a sinful creation. The sea of glass (2) also indicates God's holiness, and its mingling with fire may look to the judgment that separates people of evil from the presence of God.

How are we to handle these truths? We must seek the Spirit's help not to compromise the holiness of God. As we tell others of Christ let us not be tempted to offer platitudes and a warm comfortable feeling to any who may, perhaps even tomorrow, be facing the wrath of God with no salvation. We can learn something of this truth by singing the hymns of the Bible like this one and recognizing the deep and serious theology that they contain. In vs 3–4 the Old Testament is alluded to or quoted several times (see, for instance, Ps 111:2; Hos 14:9; Jer 10:7). This is a song for all believing people.

Note: Out of context, verse 4b might imply that all people will be saved. Not so. This looks forward to the day of victory when even his enemies will (grudgingly) have to bow down to God (see Phil 2:10).

16:1–21 The bowls of the wrath of God

Now John's vision begins to describe in detail the final judgment. It would again be wrong to suggest that there is a specific chronological order in the pouring out of these bowls of God's wrath, but their finality strikes us as we read. Take note that John does not expect us necessarily to be able to say 'Such and such has happened, therefore Christ is coming!' (15).

This chapter shows us what that final judgment will be like, and is expanded upon still further in the descriptions in chapters 17 and 18 of the judgment on the harlot and on Babylon. Though there are obvious similarities with the judgments of the trumpets and seals, there are differences too.

1. Here only those marked with the sign of the beast will be affected (2). It seems that this judgment will be observed by Christ's people who will see it as reason to praise God for his justice and judgment (5–7; remember also ch 15).

2. We are shown that the time for repentance is now passed. This point is made three times (9,11,21). They have had opportunities to repent before. Many have not taken them, and now it is too late. John shows, however, that even at the end these evil people still continue to curse God.

3. Before, only a proportion such as a third of the people or of the world has been affected, but now the effect is universal (3,4,10,20 etc).

The picture we are given is of a final and all-embracing battle between the forces of the dragon (12–16) and God himself. This is a huge spiritual battle, described in greater detail later when we shall also see how Christ himself is directly involved (eg 17:14). But God's judgment is coming now, and there is no avoiding it. In terms of what Jesus prophesied, this section seems to parallel Mark 13:24–25. The actual coming of Christ is about to happen (Mark 13:26–27).

In this passage we continue to learn about matters of eternity that we must apply to ourselves: **a)** The time for repentance will come to an end. There is no half-way house. Whose mark do we have? **b)** Are we awake, ready and dressed, or are we like Laodicea (3:17)? **c)** Let us praise God that his justice is already being seen and will be seen in how he protects us, his people, and how he judges evil.

Note: The symbolic name of 'Armageddon' may be based on Megiddo in Israel where many important battles have taken place in the past. Some suggest there will be a literal battle as ungodly kings come from the east. But the east came to be a symbol for the source of evil since it was from there that the Assyrians, Babylonians and others had come when God used them as instruments of judgment upon his people in Old Testament times.

17:1–6 Babylon the great

We noted earlier that Babylon signified 'the evil world set against God'. Many commentators have understood Babylon as a reference to Rome. The Roman Empire was persecuting Christians and even causing its emperors to be worshipped (see comments on chs 2–3). Undoubtedly the talk of seven hills (17:9), together with the evil nature of the empire and its great power around the world, would have encouraged such an identification. We must not suggest that they were wrong in making that identification, for what we have found in reading through this book is that each age can and should learn from John's vision. Other place names are also used to refer to 'the world in opposition to God' (eg 11:8), so equally we must never say 'This does *not* apply to us'.

The churches like that at Smyrna receive a message from God that tells them about their place in the world in which God is Sovereign. They are secure if they are in Christ, but judgment and tribulation continue around them. This passage therefore says the same to them as it does to us today: 'Lo, I am coming like a thief! Blessed is he who is awake' (16:15). The evil world is indeed set against God, but is now to be finally judged.

Chapters 17 and 18 give different perspectives on what has already been seen in 16:19. John stands back to see just what does happen to Babylon as the seventh bowl is poured out.

'Babylon' and 'the harlot' are identical. In these opening verses the evil world is seen to have a glory of its own. The whole vision now sets a dramatic contrast between the harlot and the woman described in ch 12. The latter was clothed with the sun and had a crown of twelve stars (12:1). Babylon is dressed in purple and scarlet, signs of great pomp and wealth (see Ezek 16:13–16), and yet she is a harlot. Once again the sexual imagery here comes from Old Testament prophetic pictures of people who forsake the God who made a covenant with them, to go after other gods.

The seductive qualities of the harlot are not to be underestimated, so John is taken by the Spirit to the wilderness to observe her, for there he is safe and protected by God (12:6,14). The full nauseating horror of what this evil world has done is seen all too vividly in v 6. The picture needs no further comment.

We Christians are often tempted to underestimate the seductiveness of the world, but when we do, the dragon is almost in sight of victory. We are sinners saved by grace, not perfect and unassailable automatons. Let us remember that even in the vision it seems that John himself would have been seduced by what he saw had he not been under the direct protection of God. The wealth and splendour of our age draws many away from the Lord. Where do we stand?

17:7–18 A mystery examined

Many people have said that this passage helps in identifying times and rulers. Some have counted seven Roman emperors and then taken the passage to refer to the myth about Nero coming back (8 – 'was, and is not and is to come', and 11). This is attractive, but even if some in the seven churches read it in that way it does not exhaust the meaning of John's vision. John's hearers 'needed to be told not *who* was reigning but his spiritual affiliations' (Sweet, p 257). This point has often been missed as scholars have concentrated on the deciphering of symbols, much of which is highly speculative.

The woman and Babylon are just one 'mystery'. Different interpretations of this passage cannot really be examined here. Some suggest that v 8 indicates that the antichrist, though having appeared before, is currently not to be seen but will come again in a final manifestation of power at the end of time. Some have tried to identify the ten kings (12) with twentieth-century powers in Europe. However, it is questionable whether we are to understand these details as having one-for-one equivalents. We have seen before that there are occasional indications of a greater, most horrific tribulation just before the day of the Lord. The theory of a coming antichrist would fit with this view. But we have questioned whether that is the way John really expects his visions to be understood. They were deeply meaningful to the seven churches and perhaps they did think of Nero as having gone and yet to return, but this would have served to keep them 'awake' for the Lord. This whole section is to teach us the same lessons (see comments on vs 1–6).

The reference to 'was, and is not . . .' probably looks to ch 12 where Satan was defeated by the crucified Christ. For those who believe, Satan 'is not' (John 12:31). However, on earth, having been thrown out of heaven, he has a limited time of limited power. Because of the power of Satan in these last days, many have been deceived into believing that the Christian faith is misplaced and irrelevant. To describe Satan as coming up (present tense – 8; 11:7) from the bottomless pit is to describe his continuing character. His nature never changes.

It is clear here that the evil of this world comes from Satan who unites all his forces to fight the Lamb, as he realizes that final judgment is coming. But as they wage war on the Lamb they in fact become divided against themselves (16). And then, without recognizing what is happening, they will unite around the beast (17). Here is a most striking glimpse of the 'mystery', that is, how God works out his plans for his people. *God*'s purposes are being carried out by the beast, kings and the harlot.

18:1–19 Babylon laid waste

This chapter now shows us the judgment (17:1) of the harlot: Babylon. It is worth looking up some of the many allusions in this passage to the prophets of the Old Testament. (Use a cross-reference edition of the Bible.)

In verses 1–3 an angel announces the falling of the city (Isa 21:9). We are reminded of some of the prophetic pronouncements of destruction on places like Assyria, Tyre and, of course, Babylon (Zeph 2:13–15; Ezek 26–27; Isa 13:19–22). She is to be left completely desolate, fit for inhabitation only by demons and foul spirits. Babylon has seduced every part of the evil world that is under Satan's domination (3).

This chapter is a chilling reminder, not just of the nature of God's judgment, but also of the danger of allowing ourselves to be taken in by what is basically evil. Particularly singled out in the vision are two areas of power which have 'committed fornication' with Babylon: **1.** government (3,9–10), and **2.** finance and trade (3,11–19). We in western Europe and North America have never in our history been so well-off. Wealth creation is a 'god' served by the vast majority of our peoples. 'Balance of payments', 'interest rates', 'inflation', 'profits', 'exchange rates', have all become common expressions used in everyday speech. Political parties all seem to have one main objective: to better the financial lot of everyone. Some may show more concern for the poor and needy than others, but always the aim is to create wealth. Court cases year after year reveal that people will lie, cheat and bribe their way into authority. Not only do many want wealth but they also want power.

We deceive ourselves if we say we are never tempted by Babylon. But vs 4–8 reveal that there is an alternative and we need to take it. God's people are to 'come out' of Babylon (Jer 50:8; 51:6–10). Here, even in the last days, Christians are reminded that they are citizens of a different city and should therefore not be caught up in the values and sins of the world around. We are to stand firm for our Lord at every point, even when this leads to the persecution and death of which we have read so much in this book. How we tackle our task in the world depends on our calling, but our values must be different and Christ-like. Glorifying and obeying God are to be our main purposes, not the creation of wealth. Serving Christ is more important than holding government power. If we are privileged to create wealth and to have power then we must use those positions not for ourselves but for God and his kingdom. We must remember that we are not to be 'yoked' with the world (2 Cor 6:14–18). For all the attractiveness of Babylon, there will be a time when it will be said of her, 'In one hour she has been laid waste' (19).

18:20–24 God's judgment

Earth has become the scene of great tragedy, and yet in this book we have become accustomed, from time to time, to returning to the praises that continue for ever in the presence of God. Verse 20 sounds almost callous to our ears, and yet we must remember what we have learned earlier from John. The gospel message involves the proclaiming of God's universal kingship and sovereignty. We have come to understand that just as we wish to see God vindicate his name, so we seek to see all evil destroyed.

Heaven now rejoices because the longed-for hour has come. Evil is being destroyed. God has passed judgment in favour of the righteous. The very ones who have been so tortured and oppressed by Babylon now find themselves rejoicing with those in heaven as God's perfect justice is done.

Verses 21–24 describes the desolation of this once great city. Talking of this chapter Rushdoony has said (p 198), 'The grand design of man is to create a paradise without God, a perfect world in terms of total self-affirmation. To this purpose the politics of man are bent, and to this goal he bends every effort.' Here the end of such designs is described symbolically (see the whole of Jer 50–51, but especially 51:61–64). The reference to a 'millstone' perhaps recalls the words of Jesus who, talking to the powers and authorities of his day, said, 'Whoever causes one of these little ones who believe in me to sin, it would be better for him to have a great millstone fastened round his neck and to be drowned in the depth of the sea' (Matt 18:6).

The examples used to demonstrate the completeness of the destruction also derive from the Old Testament (eg Jer 25:10; Ezek 26:13) and are worthy of note. Culture, art, technology, financial trading and even social relationships are all mentioned in these verses. Just as for a Christian there should be no area of life that is not totally committed to the Kingdom of God, so we find that there is no area of life that is not fully committed to Babylon by those whom she has seduced. Here is a most serious warning for those who think they can come to a compromise with the world, or who would try to separate what they do at work or for relaxation from what they say in their creeds and at church.

The chapter concludes with what seems almost paradoxical. The blood of those slain on earth is found in Babylon when her destruction is seen, and yet it is the blood of those who are currently rejoicing in heaven (20). The suffering and tribulation which they have been put through by Babylon has not been wasted. The ones who seemed to have nothing and who gave up even what they had, have finally come into their inheritance.

19:1–10 Praise the Lord!

What a contrast there is between these verses and chapter 18! The wailing of the kings, the weeping of the merchants and the crying of the shipmasters, have given way to great praises of God. What was presaged in 18:20 is now seen in all its glory.

'Hallelujah'. This word is a transliteration of the Hebrew word meaning 'praise Jahweh'. It is found nowhere else in the New Testament, but is used in several psalms in the Old Testament (eg Ps 111:1; 112:1). We have glimpsed this type of praise earlier, but now that the fall of Babylon has taken place it is more extended and the whole of heaven is seen to participate.

The first 'great multitude' perhaps refers to the angel throngs, and mention is made again of the twenty-four elders and four living creatures (4) for they are also part of this praise. The call from the throne (5) may come from one of those living creatures calling for God to be praised. The second 'great multitude' may include the redeemed who are also now before the throne. Whether John is hearing distinct groups is not important. The vision is one of heaven itself in which all, without exception, are worshipping God for the salvation he has brought.

We have here a very helpful example of how to praise God – an ability that often seems to be missing these days. Our praise is based on the fact that God has worked in history. Therefore we should meditate on his works, remembering how much there is for which to give thanks and praise. The multitude rehearse what God has just done (2,3,8). They praise him for his salvation, glory, power, his righteous judgments, his kingly rule, the marriage of the Lamb and the presentation of the bride. 'Salvation' reminds us of the whole purposes of God for his people, although primarily it recalls the recent salvation of the people from the wrath of God and his judgment on the world. Thinking about God's work in our own lives and the salvation that is ours will open up for us great areas of praise and thanksgiving.

The wedding feast of the Lamb. The image of marriage between God and his people has its roots in the Old Testament, especially Ezekiel 16:8–14. Jesus used the idea in some of the parables about the kingdom (Matt 25:1–13). The contrast between the beautiful, chaste bride (the church) and the harlot (Babylon) is obvious. The bride's 'righteous deeds' (8) have not earned her this position but were 'granted her'. God even gave the church her dress (see Eph 2:8–10)!

It is strange that after such a clear vision John should be tempted himself to worship one who is not God (10). Perhaps the lesson here that John had to learn abruptly was of particular benefit to those in the church of his day who were tempted to worship angels. Only God is to be worshipped.

19:11–21 Faithful and True

At last the second coming of Jesus is described. The book of visions has come to its great climax. Babylon's destruction has been announced. The bride is ready. Christ comes seated on a white horse. It is clear that it is Christ who is being described because of the names attributed to him.

1. 'Faithful and True' (11) recalls the name given to Jesus as he addresses the Laodiceans (3:14). It reminds us that God is faithful to the covenant and that Christ returns as the covenant Lord.

2. 'The Word of God' (13) draws attention to the fact that Christ actively carries out the Father's will. In John 1:1 the same idea emphasizes Christ's creative action. Here the emphasis is more on his judging and destructive action. Verse 15, drawing on Isaiah 11:4, also finds a reflection in Hebrews 4:12–13.

3. 'Kings of kings and Lord of lords' (16) is a name proclaimed on the most visible part of the rider's body. The absolute rule and dominion of Christ is manifest to all. The name was mentioned in 17:14 where the faithful elect come with the conquering Lamb. This indicates, probably, that the 'armies of heaven' referred to in v 14 are also the faithful saints.

What follows is a horrific description of the wrath of God the Almighty (15), as it is poured out on all who have followed the beast and received his mark. This judgment is described in terms of war, and yet we know that the battle has already been won on the cross and in the resurrection. What is happening here is that the final judgment is being described vividly in terms of war, battle and defeat of the enemy. This is not a straightforward battle, it has to do with God's law-court. Here is the just penalty being inflicted on all who have, down the ages, sought to fight against God and Christ. Ezekiel 39:4–6 provides the background for the description of judgment.

The 'lake of fire' is a metaphor for total, eternal and irrevocable judgment. Other terms, equally horrific, describe this punishment elsewhere in the New Testament (eg Matt 25:30). In suggesting that such descriptions are metaphorical let us be extremely careful not to mitigate the nature of this eternal punishment. The fact of the matter is that hell is so dreadful and final that only metaphorical language can communicate anything of its nature.

The greatest of all days has been described, and yet the description has not been altogether pleasant. Let us be thankful that if we know and love the Lord, if we believe that he has shed his blood for us (13), then we have been sealed with his mark and will be vindicated on that day. Let us be encouraged also to use the time that remains before Christ's return to tell many others of the salvation to be found in the Messiah Saviour.

Questions for further study and discussion on Revelation 14–19

1. Which do you find the greater temptation: to compromise with the world or to opt out of the world? How can such temptation be overcome?

2. What is the content of the 'eternal gospel' the angel proclaims (14:6)? Can we identify with the praise of the crowds mentioned in 14:1–5?

3. What more can be learned from 15:3–4 about how to praise God? Can you think of any hymns or choruses you sing which contain all the elements of this biblical song? If not, what do you feel it says about your worship?

4. Looking at 16:1–21, what does judgment mean for you personally?

5. How exactly do you see the talk of 'Babylon the great' (17:1–6) applying to your own situation? Are you seduced?

6. Can you see ways today in which God's divine sovereignty overrules the work of Satan? Do you find this a source of encouragement?

7. Think again about your answers to question 5 above. Then examine how you can best ensure that you have 'come out' from Babylon. What does this mean in practice?

8. How do modern politics reflect 'the grand design of man . . . to create a paradise without God'?

9. Spend some time examining what 'salvation' has meant to you personally. Imagine the 'wedding feast'. Then praise the Lord using the words of praise in 19:1–8.

10. What do you look forward to most in the second coming? Are you at all apprehensive?

20:1–10 A thousand years
(Part 1)

In ch 20 the devil is bound and thrown into the pit. Saints are resurrected and reign with Christ for 1000 years. After this period of time Satan will again be loosed to deceive the nations. Those who follow Satan then march on the church (those in the 'beloved city' – 9) and the final eternal judgment of Satan takes place.

We have deliberately taken the book of Revelation one step at a time up to this point and have found that it has proved intelligible and has challenged us in all sorts of ways. Now, although space prohibits any detail, it is worth examining chapters 19 and 20 from the three perspectives mentioned in the Introduction (p 77).

Pre-millennialism There are many variants within this position. It is insisted that ch 20 follows ch 19 chronologically in *history*. Christ returns (ch 19), the righteous dead are raised and rule with him for 1000 years (20:1–6), before 'the rest of the dead' (those who are not Christ's) are raised for the final judgment (7–15). This millennium will show the rule of King Jesus, the fulfilment of covenant promises and will demonstrate that a city ruled by Christ faces no threat even from a 'loosed' Satan. Some pre-millennialists prefer to see the '1000' as a symbol describing the fulness of the time rather than its extent. Some 'Dispensationalists' see this rule entirely in terms of a restored *national* Israel with Christ at its head.

Post-millennialism This view suggests that ch 19 has not actually described the second coming, but rather is symbolic of the way the church, under Christ's lordship, regains the world for the Lord. Once this is done Christ returns to raise the dead and judge and bind Satan and his followers. Thereafter, heaven and earth are re-created for Christ and his people.

Amillennialism This position tends to see ch 20 as a recapitulation of all that has gone so far. There is no actual period of rule as seen in the other views. Rather, 1000 is regarded as a symbol (see Introduction). Satan was bound by Jesus (Mark 3:27; Luke 10:18), and the reign of Christ is proclaimed through his church throughout the ages, for the saints are *now* 'raised' and seated 'in the heavenly places' with Christ (Eph 2:6). The first resurrection is conversion (John 5:25). The second is for the judgment day.

It is a sad fact that Christians have often divided somewhat acrimoniously over these issues that should be matters of the greatest rejoicing for all of us. Whatever position we take, we should always bear in mind the *function* of John's message here which is to continue to give joy and comfort to Christians in the present, even if the events he describes are future. On the next page this commentary takes its stand on a basically amillennialist position, although it is recognized that some of the arguments for other perspectives are also very persuasive.

20:1–10 A thousand years
(Part 2)

John does not place this vision in a time relationship with ch 19. He simply says, 'And I saw . . .' (not 'then' – RSV, 1,4). God has complete control over Satan, for the period of his binding is entirely in God's hands. The binding took place during the earthly life of the King of kings (Mark 3:27). Numbers are used metaphorically in this book. Here ten to the power of three (1000) indicates God's perfection in setting, but limiting, the time.

This passage now gloriously recapitulates the theme of Revelation: that the church is preserved by God and is sealed for protection against Satan, who will ultimately be destroyed. While being preserved, the church reigns with Christ for this limited period of the last days before the second coming. There is also a marvellous vision of encouragement to those who will suffer death, for they are seen also to be with Christ. Satan has not triumphed but the saints have conquered (2:10; 12:11; see also Dan 7:18). Regarding the 'first resurrection' (5,6), look again at Ephesians 2:6 where the idea of resurrection clearly refers to conversion, which results in being seated with Christ 'in the heavenly places'. The 'second death' looks to the final judgment – never to be experienced by those raised with Christ.

The vision of vs 7–10 continues the recapitulation. Now we see again the great battle in which God's judgment is described. With Christ in control of the church the saints have nothing to fear even from Satan's last great effort (see Rom 8:38–39). Chapter 20 now makes it clear that not just beast and prophet but Satan himself is thrown into the lake of fire for ever. Reference to Gog and Magog in v 8 also suggests that we are right in assuming that this chapter is a recapitulation for we have seen that great judgment already referred to in 19:17–18 (see Ezek 38 and 39).

Satan is more clearly manifested at some times in history than at other times. Similarly, the victory of the saints 'seated in the heavenly places' is clearer at some times than at other times as they seek to bring God's rule to the present age. But the final judgment day is not to be like the other ups and downs of a battle with a Satan who has been 'bound'. The final battle will see Satan in all his power trying to fend off the judgment of the Almighty. The victory won on the cross will be established.

Surely the point of this is to give the church the ultimate and total comfort that, whatever appearances may be, for Christians there is no need to fear this judgment of which so much has been heard. In fact they are reigning with Christ, and are his priests (1:6; 1 Pet 2:9). The covenant promises of peace and victory have not been forgotten. There is an absolute assurance that when this period is over Satan and his followers will be punished.

20:11–14 The judgment throne

Whatever our understanding of the millennium these verses return us to common ground with most commentators. Here is a description of the final judgment. The glory of God is associated with the throne that is 'great' and 'white'. It causes everything else to fade into insignificance. For a brief moment it seems as though nothing else exists at all, but then John sees the dead standing before the throne.

It is suggested that the dead here are only those who have continued to rebel against God and are being raised for their condemnation. If the 'first resurrection' of the previous chapter was for Christians, then obviously this would be the case. But we have argued that the first resurrection was a metaphor for conversion, in which case there is good reason for seeing this as the general resurrection of all people who have died, so that all should be judged for both good and evil. Certainly elsewhere in the New Testament it seems this is the picture of the final resurrection day (2 Cor 5:10; Rom 14:10–12; 1 Cor 1:8).

Judgment of the resurrected dead takes place by reading two books. Again metaphorical language is being used, but the idea is clear. Judgment is based on what is in the books and on works (12; see Dan 7:10). This does present some difficulty since we know that we are saved not by works but by grace through faith. Can it possibly be that the Lamb's 'book of life' actually contains a record of our deeds? There is a tension here in the pictures being described though no real conflict exists.

It is quite possible to see the judgment from two perspectives. On the one hand there is the final and irrevocable writing of names in the 'book of life'. If a person's name is there then they are saved from the wrath of God. The other books list the deeds of all. God's final justice is seen to be perfect. If names are in the Lamb's book of life then the deeds listed beside those names (or perhaps in the other books) will be the righteous deeds of the saints – not because they were without unrighteous deeds, but because those have already been dealt with on the cross and Christ's righteousness is imputed to those who have faith (2 Cor 5:21; Phil 3:9). On the other hand the unrighteous will find that, as the book is opened, they cannot escape the awesome righteousness of God's judgment which shows up every single detail of their sin. There will be no doubt in anyone's mind on that day that justice has been done.

What joy there is as, finally, Death and Hades are destroyed. Here they are personified. At last death, the great curse (Gen 3), has been removed. Eternal death was removed on the cross for believers (2 Tim 1:10), but here preparation is being made for the new heaven and earth, and the final enemy to be conquered is physical death, for the righteous will now live for ever (1 Cor 15:25–26).

21:1–8 New heaven and new earth

The last two chapters of this book are among the most glorious in all Scripture. Finally the goal of creation is realized – perfect harmony and obedience to the creator. Here all the symptoms and results of sin and the curse of God are gone (4). Not only will the earth be new, but heaven will be too. Symbols such as the sea, indicating separation from God, will no longer exist. Now God will dwell with men (3).

All the prophecies revealed by God through the ages finally find total fulfilment. It is one of the most marvellous joys of our present Christian lives to see how God's word, delivered over such great periods of history, hangs together, being utterly faithful and utterly true. Here at the end of Revelation and, most appropriately, at the end of our Bibles, the whole of God's word is drawn together. Compare, for example, the following: Isaiah 65:17–19; 2 Peter 3:11–13; Hebrews 11:8–10; 12:22–24; Isaiah 7:14; 8:10; Leviticus 26:11–13; Ezekiel 37:24–27. Notice also how Christians experience the first-fruits of much of this even now. We know God to be dwelling among men now, in Jesus Christ (John 1:14). We experience something of the marriage relationship (Eph 5:29–33). Being in Christ we know something of the 'new creation' (2 Cor 5:17; Gal 6:15–16), and have already tasted the water of life (John 4:10,13–14; see Isa 55:1).

Some people spend much time discussing the nature of the new heaven and earth, and draw unnecessarily sharp distinctions between the recreation of a new earth (Eden restored) and the emphasis on the New Jerusalem. Some say that they are a 'spiritual' reality and not at all material. But this seems to miss the point of John's vision. As we have seen from the verses above, the new heavens, earth and Jerusalem all fulfil many different aspects of prophecy and we should not exclude or emphasize one in favour of another.

It is worth mentioning here that the Bible never talks of these new entities in terms of the soul 'escaping' this world. Rather, resurrected *bodies/people* are given a new place to live. 'Throughout the entire Bible, the ultimate destiny of God's people is an earthly destiny ... biblical thought always places man on a redeemed earth, not in a heavenly realm removed from earthly existence' (Ladd). So what is the relationship between the old and the new? Paul describes this by way of an analogy involving the seed and ear of wheat (1 Cor 15:37–38). There is real continuity between the first and the second state, but the second is inconceivably more glorious. Just as there is continuity between the old and the new covenants, between Jesus before his death and after his bodily resurrection, so there is between the old and new earth, heaven and Jerusalem. But for now we can only describe this with John's symbols of beauty, great value and glory.

21:9–27 The New Jerusalem

This section introduces in more detail the New Jerusalem mentioned in v 2. The contrast with the harlot (17:1) is stressed by the very words used. The bride is now described as a city having the radiance of the glory of God (11). This is the true beauty of the church, built upon the foundational teaching of the prophets and apostles (12,14). Again we already know in the present something of all this (Eph 2:19–22), but one day we will experience it in its fulness.

The picture that is built up here, as with so many others in this book, is derived from Ezekiel's prophecy. (See Ezek 40:2; 45:1; 48:31–35.) The measurements of the city are obviously symbolic, showing it to be cube-shaped and about 1500 miles in each direction. The perfection of this city is without question. The time for which Paul said he and 'the whole creation' were longing has arrived: everything has been set free from bondage to decay, and the full adoption and inheritance of the sons is now seen (Rom 8:18–23). Isaiah 60 also provides background, especially for vs 22–27.

There is so much for us to learn here. Christians comprise the church. All who have faith are the 'bride', and the citizens of this new city. The promises of this section are as relevant for us today as they were for the seven churches who originally received the book.

1. Are we prepared, in order to ensure that we inherit these blessings, to be on our guard against false apostles laying a false foundation (2:2)?

2. We are the bride of Christ. Do we love as we did at the start of the relationship, or will we not take part in the coming of the bride (2:4)?

3. We have a foretaste of 'God with us' as Christ 'walks among the lampstands' (1:13; 2:1). We should savour and enjoy the experience so much now that we look forward with even greater expectation to the New Jerusalem.

4. The people at Philadelphia are exhorted to 'hold fast' what they have (3:11–12), so they will be pillars 'in the temple of God'. The name of the New Jerusalem will be on them, indicating that they belong for ever to that city.

As with those early churches, our temptation today is to neglect the apostolic doctrine and compromise the truth. We must walk in the light now if we are ever to enjoy the wonders of the new creation. Even here in these last verses of the book the gospel challenge comes through to us strongly. We look forward with joy to the time when the redeemed of all nations will come together needing no temple and no further light, because the Father and the Lamb are there in the midst of us.

22:1–5 The Garden and the City

Earlier it was said that people often try to drive a wedge between prophecies describing a restoration of Eden and the New Jerusalem. That such a view is misplaced is obvious in 21:19–21 where the foundations of the city are adorned with stones that Ezekiel symbolically tells us also adorned the Garden of Eden (see Ezek 28:13–14). In these first five verses it is again evident that two strands of prophecy come together. The bride comes to a new heaven and earth; the city comes down from heaven to a new earth made ready for her.

In a real way the paradise of Eden is now re-established, and yet what is now received is even greater than Eden ever was, for the Lamb is also in the Garden, and men and women have known the fulness of the grace of God in a way that Adam and Eve never knew.

Drawing on Ezekiel again (47:1–12), John describes a river. In Ezekiel it flows from the temple, but here there is no temple. Rather it flows directly from the throne of God which is now the city's focal point. (Note how here in v1 and in 21:22 God and the Lamb are put together, indicating the deity of Christ.) John's vision merges the ideas of Ezekiel with the view received of the river in the Garden of Eden (Gen 2:8–10). The curse of the Garden has clearly been overturned in the destruction of death and of Satan. Where once the Garden had been inaccessible, now its great blessings flow out freely to all people everywhere. The river of the Garden brings life, just as the fruit of the tree of life is now available to all the nations, that is to all redeemed people from all the lands of earth. The curse has gone. Genesis 3:16–24 is forgotten and left behind (3a; see Zech 14:11).

Just as was once true in the Garden, the fullest possible relationship with God will be restored. But eternity is even greater than Eden which was, in effect, a physical prophecy of the new heaven and the new earth. The people of the city will drink waters of life and eat fruit of life. They will know moment by moment that all these blessings come directly from God, just as the river flows now from God's throne. Even the light will now come directly from God. Every warning, every encouragement, every pleading of God with his people down through the ages that they should recognize that he supplies all their needs is now written into everyday life and missed by no one. No longer will people need to learn that 'man lives by everything that proceeds out of the mouth of the Lord', but they will see it and know it and live with the truth day by day as they look on the Lord's face (Deut 8:3; Neh 9:20,26; 1 Cor 10:3–5). Have we learned the lesson of Deuteronomy 8:3 yet? The gospel of Christ gives us a foretaste here and now of all these blessings of eternity.

22:6–15 I am coming soon

In the closing verses of this book John sees and hears words that are particularly to be applied to the seven churches, and thus to the whole church through the ages. The message of the previous twenty-one chapters has become obvious as those visions have been studied, and here its implications for the present are made abundantly clear.

All that has been said is true, for the words of the one who is Faithful and True are 'trustworthy' (6,16; 19:11; 3:14). John insists that this work is a genuine prophecy and that the events recounted are happening soon (6; 1:3). Just as happened in 19:10 John's response is to fall down and worship the angel who has mediated much of the information to him. John has seen so much, and yet he is so obviously human in succumbing to the temptation to worship a lesser – though glorious – being than God. (See comments on 19:10.)

The Lord is returning soon to bring the wages. Meanwhile, there is time to obey the words of the prophecy (7,10–12). Here we are reminded of what we should do:

1. We must worship God. How often do we offer praise and thanks in the wrong direction when we have been very moved by what we have seen or heard? It is so easy to set a great preacher, theologian of the past or Christian 'pop-star' on a pedestal, and forget that the message he brings is not his but God's. Is the communicator of the message more highly thought of, in our era of mass communication, than the one about whom the messenger speaks? John's problem still exists today as some people look to angels, or other humans whom they consider to be 'saints', and bow before them rather than before the Lord Christ whom the angels and 'saints' serve. John had to be reprimanded again (9;19:10). We too must worship God alone.

2. As the 'righteous' we must do right. This may sound obvious, but it is foolish to think that we might be immune from the temptations and trials which have been described in this book in detail.

3. We must be holy (11). Here the emphasis is on the separation from the world demanded of those who belong to Christ and who are set apart for the service of God (see 1 Peter 2:11–12).

4. Above all, Christians must 'wash their robes' (14) if they are to be 'blessed' (to receive God's covenant mercies). In order to come to the tree of life, it is necessary to know that Jesus died for us and to identify with and believe in that death. Saving faith saves for ever because God has sealed his saints to himself, but day by day as his children we will need to turn back to him in repentance asking for the forgiveness available through the shed blood of Jesus. This is our access to the city: through Christ the redeemer. All others are outside.

22:16–21 Come, Lord Jesus!

The date of the return of Christ is not known, but it is the constant cry of the church that the King should come so that she may enjoy for ever all the blessings that this prophecy has outlined. Notice that the Holy Spirit prompts the church (the bride) to make the prayer (17), and Christ replies in verse 20. Some suggest that verse 17 is an evangelistic appeal. This seems unlikely as the whole book is addressed to the churches, and verse 17 seems to complement verses 12 and 20, rather than introducing a different subject. However, some may be like the Laodicean church members. Let *them* come to Christ (see comments on 3:20).

The modern church seems to react in two different but equally wrong ways to these teachings about the return of Christ. Some virtually ignore all such texts in Scripture, especially the book of Revelation. They believe in the return, but rarely if ever pray for it, and it does not seem to impinge on their day-to-day lives. Others are chiefly preoccupied with chronological details and forget that no one knows the hour of the return. While looking for the fulfilment of all the details they fail to use this age correctly, and so do not '*keep* the words' of the book (7)!

All should heed the dire warning in verses 18–19 against tampering with the prophecy. The sovereign covenant Lord, whose word cannot be changed, has spoken. No one may decide to take note of only parts of this work and neglect or ignore other parts. It is all too easy to feel the exhilaration in chapters 21 and 22, but totally ignore the implications of passages like ch 16. No one should be involved in contrary teaching, either by adding his own supposed visions or by subtracting from the totality of this message.

Unlike some of the apocalyptic literature of John's time, this prophecy is open. The words are not to be 'sealed up' (10). This is a 'testimony for the churches' from and about the King. Christ's words that he is from David's line (16) stress that the covenantal promises made to David are fulfilled in Christ, who rules for ever and whose kingdom is established (2 Sam 7:12–14a). He judges perfectly (Isa 11:1–5), and he upholds his people (Isa 9:6–7). Just as the whole of the vision has centred on this kingship of God and Christ, so the gospel that is preached today should centre on his rule.

In this prophecy the kingship of God over all the world (rebellious and believing) has been taught. The gospel calls believers to make sure that they recognize Christ's kingship in every area of life at all times.

Questions for further study and discussion on Revelation 20–22

1. List some of the biblical promises of covenant peace and victory which are true now for all believers.

2. Is your name in the Lamb's book of life? How do you know?

3. Spend time reviewing all the references to the Old Testament mentioned in the comments on 21:1–8.

4. In what ways is apostolic doctrine neglected these days?

5. Meditate on the blessings of the re-established Eden. What do you most look forward to?

6. How do we gain access to the city?
What do suffering, and our attitude to it, have to do with the return of the Lord?

7. In which areas of your life do you not recognize Christ's kingship? What will you do about it?

Suggestions for further reading

Berkouwer, G C   *The Return of Christ*. Grand Rapids: W B Eerdmans, 1972.

Dumbrell, W J   *The End of the Beginning. Revelation 21–22 and the Old Testament*. Exeter: Paternoster, 1985.

Gundry, R H   *A Survey of the New Testament* (revised edition). Grand Rapids: Zondervan, 1981.

Morris, L   *The Revelation of St John*. Leicester: IVP, reprinted 1983.

Mounce, R H   *The Book of Revelation*. Grand Rapids: W B Eerdmans, 1977.

Wilcock, M   *The Message of Revelation*. Leicester: IVP, 1975.

Select bibliography

1 and 2 Peter and Jude

Bauckham, R J   *Jude, 2 Peter*. Waco, Texas: Word Books, 1983.

Cranfield, C E B   *1 and II Peter and Jude*. London: SCM, 1960.

Green, M   *2 Peter and Jude*. London: The Tyndale Press, 1968.

Kelly, J N D   *The Epistles of Peter and Jude*. London: A and C Black, 1969.

Moule, C F D   'The Nature and Purpose of 1 Peter' in *New Testament Studies* Vol III, No 1 (November, 1956), pp 1–11.

Selwyn, E G   *The First Epistle of St. Peter*. London: Macmillan, 1947.

Stibbs, A M   *The First Epistle General of Peter*. London: IVP, 1959.

The letters of John

Brown, R E   *The Epistles of John*. London: Geoffrey Chapman, 1983.

Ellis, E E   *The World of St John*. Exeter: Paternoster, 1984.

Guthrie, D   *New Testament Introduction*. Leicester: IVP, 1970.

Kistemaker, S   *James and I–III John*. Grand Rapids: Baker Book House, 1986.

Marshall, I H   *The Epistles of John*. Grand Rapids: W B Eerdmans, 1978.

Smalley, S S   *1, 2, 3 John*. Waco, Texas: Word Books, 1984.

Stott, J W R   *The Epistles of John*. London: The Tyndale Press, 1964.

Revelation

Caird, G B   *The Revelation of St John the Divine*. London: A and C Black, 1966.

Hemer, C J   *The Letters to the seven Churches of Asia in their Local Setting*. Sheffield: JSOT Press, 1986.

Ladd, G E   *A Commentary on the Revelation of John*. Grand Rapids: W B Eerdmans, 1972.

Rushdoony, R J   *Thy Kingdom Come. Studies in Daniel and Revelation*. New Jersey: Presbyterian and Reformed, 1971.

Sweet, J   *Revelation*. London: SCM, 1979.